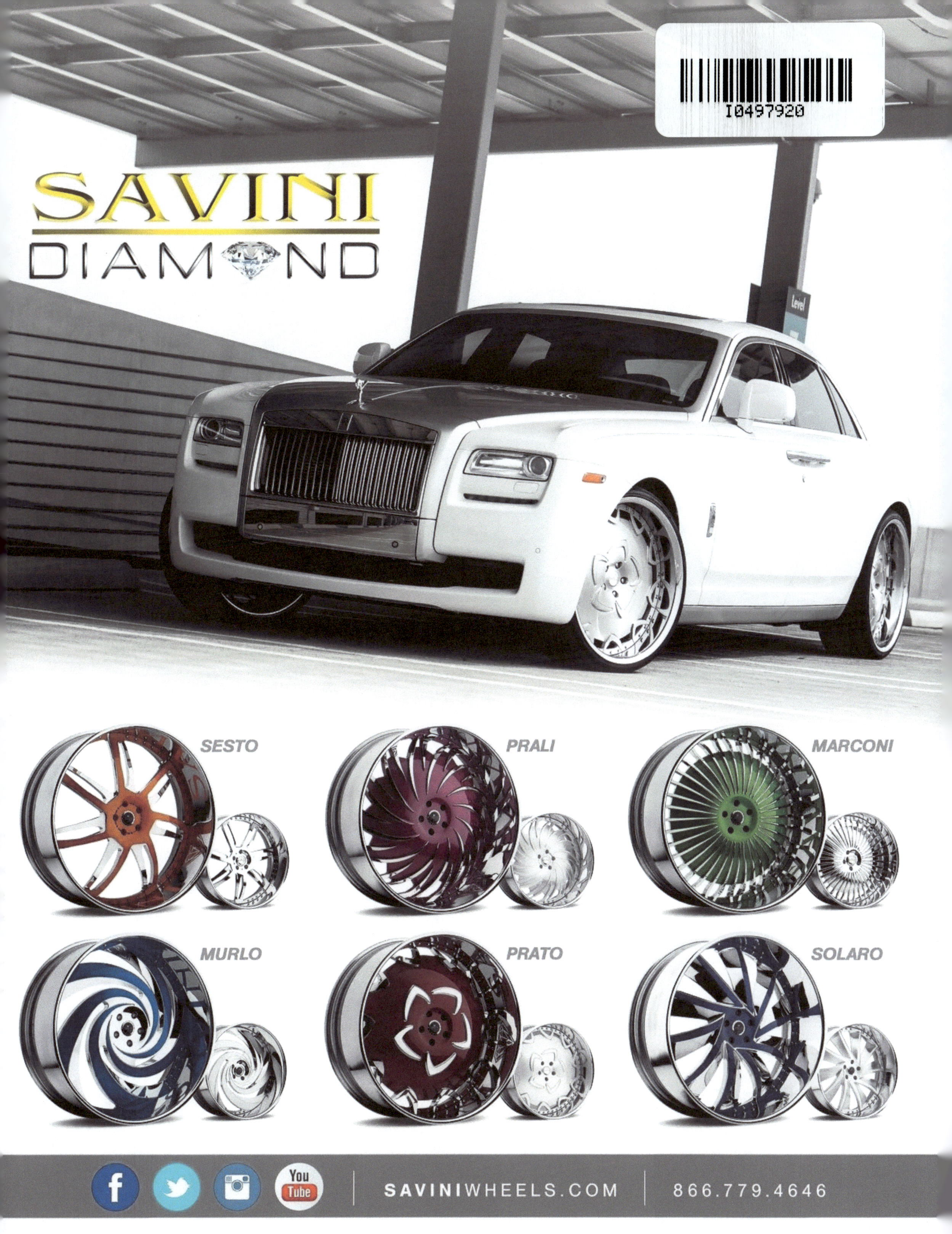

SAVINI DIAMOND

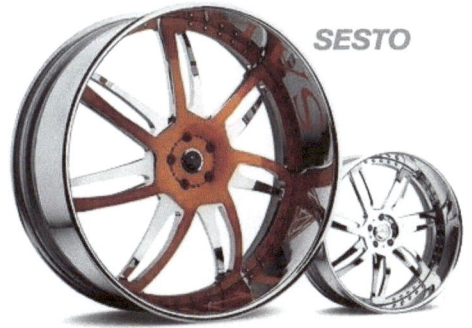 SESTO

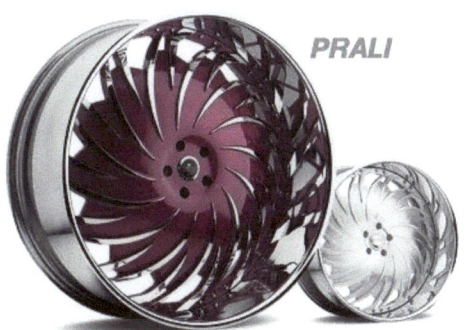 PRALI

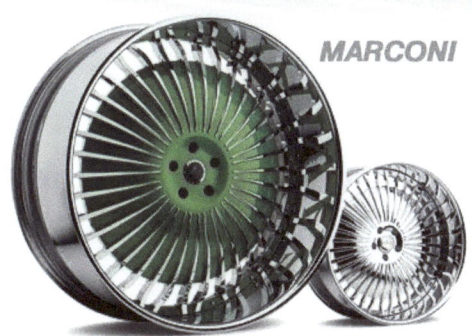 MARCONI

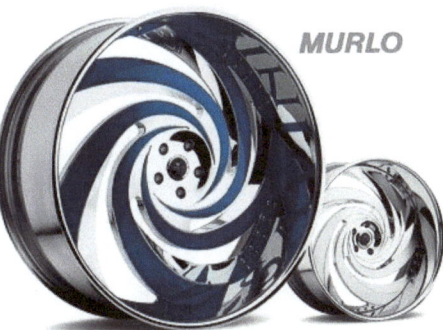 MURLO

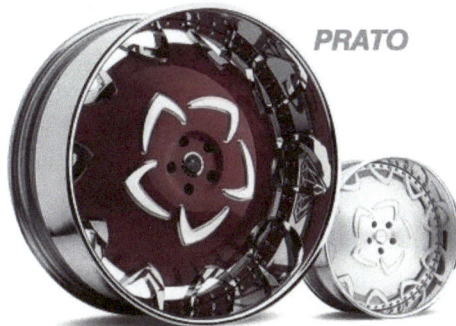 PRATO

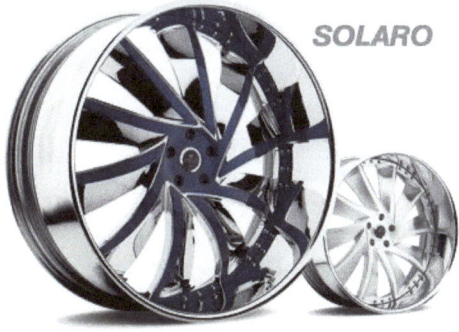 SOLARO

SAVINIWHEELS.COM | 866.779.4646

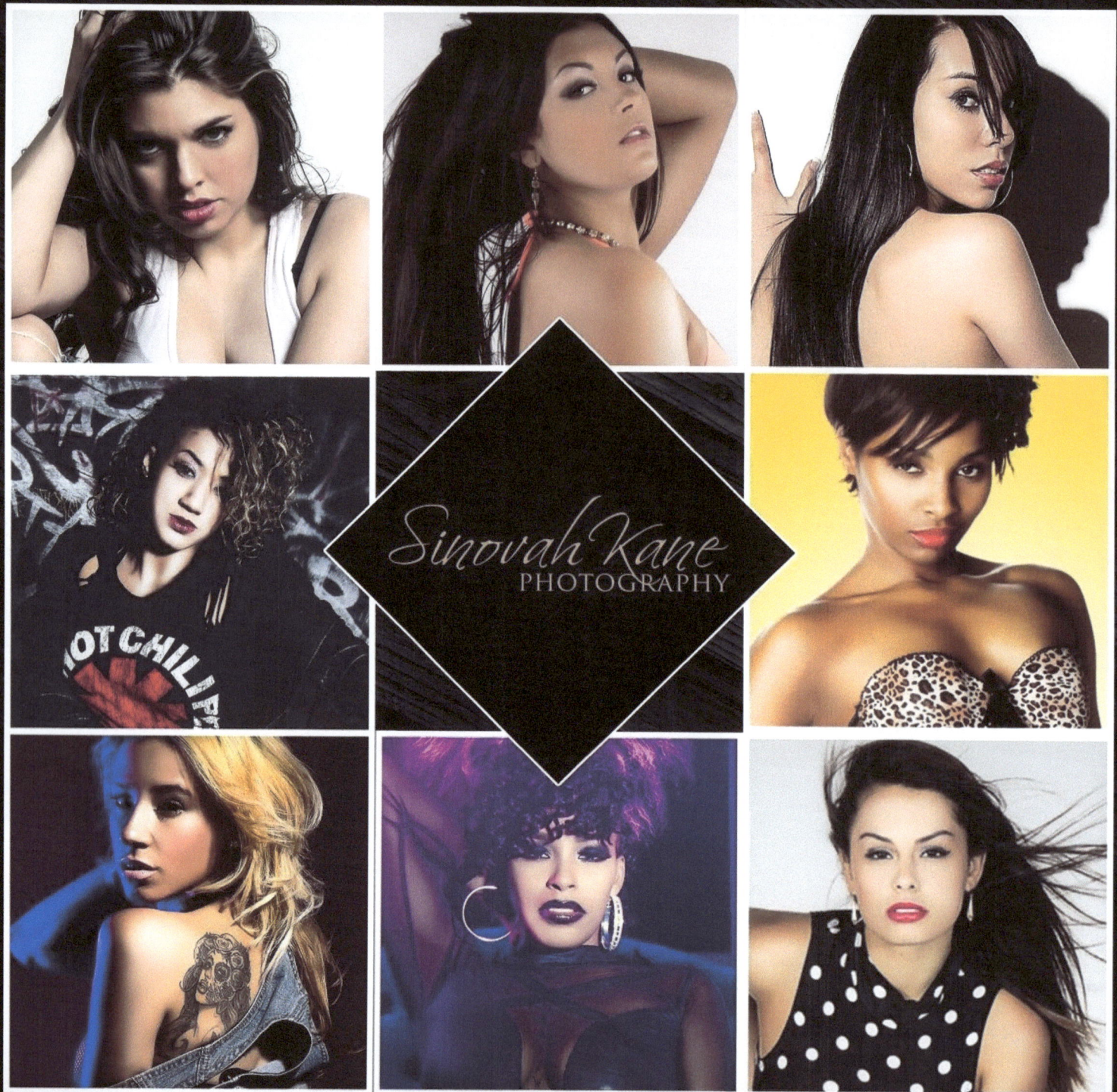

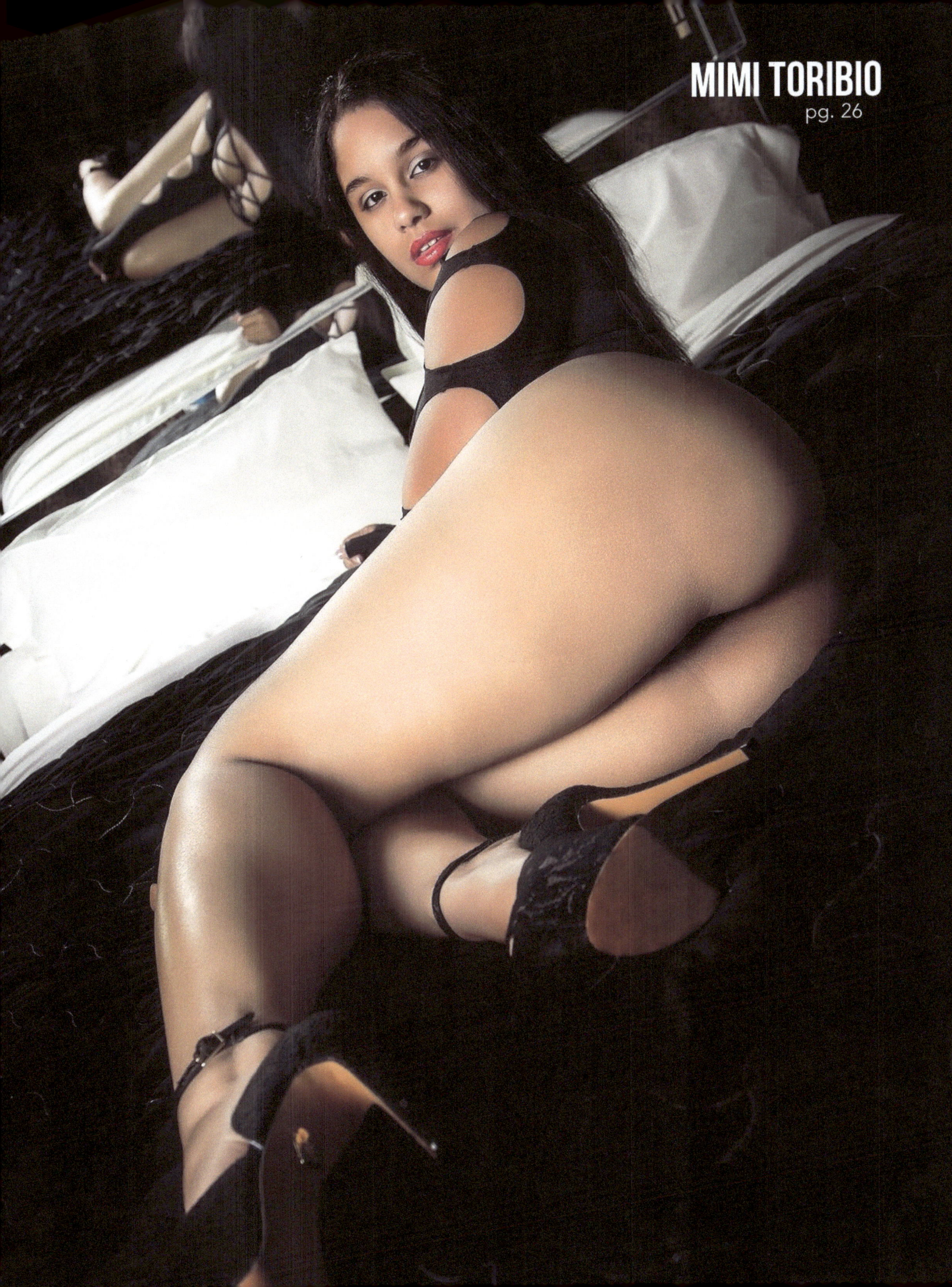

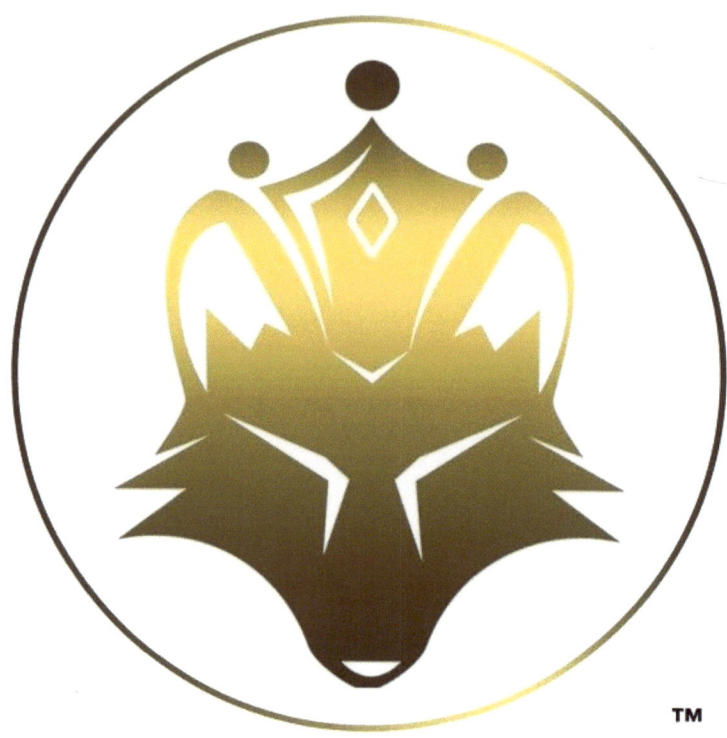

WWW.FOXTAILMAG.COM

FOXTAIL Magazine (ISSN #978-1720-388500), Issue #5 (May 2016), is published bi-monthly by **Foxtail, Inc.**, 945 W. Agatite Ave., Chicago, IL 60640. The subscription rate is $24.95 per year. One-year subscriptions rates: U.S., $24.95; Canada, $54.95; for all other countries, $84.95 in prepaid U.S. funds. Periodicals postage paid at Chicago, IL and additional mailing offices. POSTMASTER: Send address changes to *FOXTAIL Magazine,* 945 W. Agatite Ave., Chicago, IL 60640,. Reproduction or use of any part of Issue #5 (May 2016) of *FOXTAIL Magazine* without the written consent of the publisher is prohibited. Return postage must accompany all manuscripts, drawings or photographs. All manuscripts, drawings or photographs sent to *FOXTAIL Magazine* will be treated as unconditionally assigned for publication and copyright purposes and are subject to the magazine's right to edit and comment editorially. *FOXTAIL Magazine* assumes no responsibility for the advertisements made herein or the quality and availability of the products advertised herein. *FOXTAIL Magazine* assumes no responsibility to determine whether the people whose photographs or statements appear in such advertisements have, in fact, endorsed such products or consented to the use of their names or photographs, or the statements attributed to them. The publisher is exempt from the record-keeping requirements and disclosure statements mandated by 18 U.S. Code, Section 2257 A - C and the pertinent regulations, 28 C.F.R. Ch.1, Part 75, since all of such material falls within the exempted material set forth in Section 75(a) (1-3) of the regulations.

For Advertising Information Contact:
Foxtail Magazine
945 W. Agatite Ave.
Chicago, IL 60640-4044
advertising@foxtailmag.com

FOXTAIL

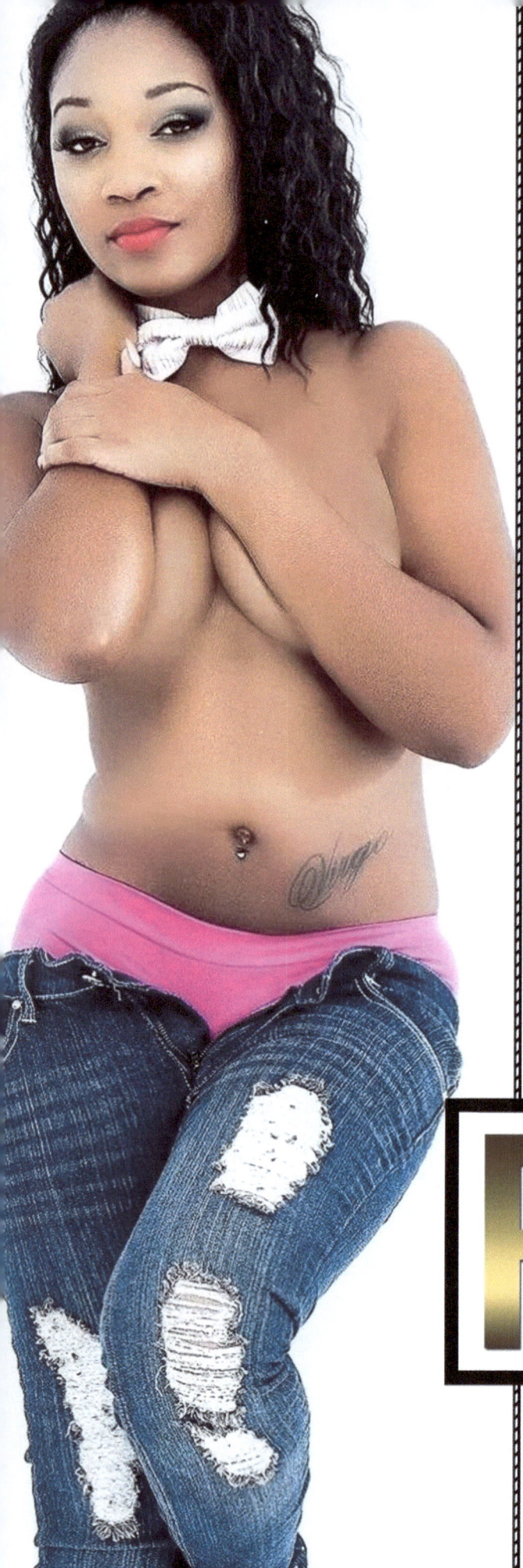

MODEL | BELLA NYKOLE PG. 42

FOXTAIL MAGAZINE
BEAUTY IS LIFE, AND LIFE IS BEAUTIFUL

EDITOR-IN-CHIEF
Charles C. Rigby II

ASSISTANT EDITOR
Tony Rudd

SENIOR PHOTOGRAPHY
Sinovah Kane

GRAPHIC DESIGN/PHOTO EDITING
Sinovah Kane Studios

WRITING STAFF
ChristopherSmith
Irene Lankin-Duffy
Berber Ormeling
Tony ngelhart
Viola Irvin
Arthur Thares
Clara Freeman
Josh Durso

PHOTOGRAPHY
Martell Jr. Photograpy
Sinovah Kane
Myron Vines
Brandon Foster
Nelson O. Smith
Jova Films

FOXTAIL MAGAZINE

WWW.FOXTAILMAG.COM

CONTACT
info@foxtailmag.com
modeling@foxtailmag.com
submissions@foxtailmag.com

TABLE OF CONTENTS

ISSUE #5

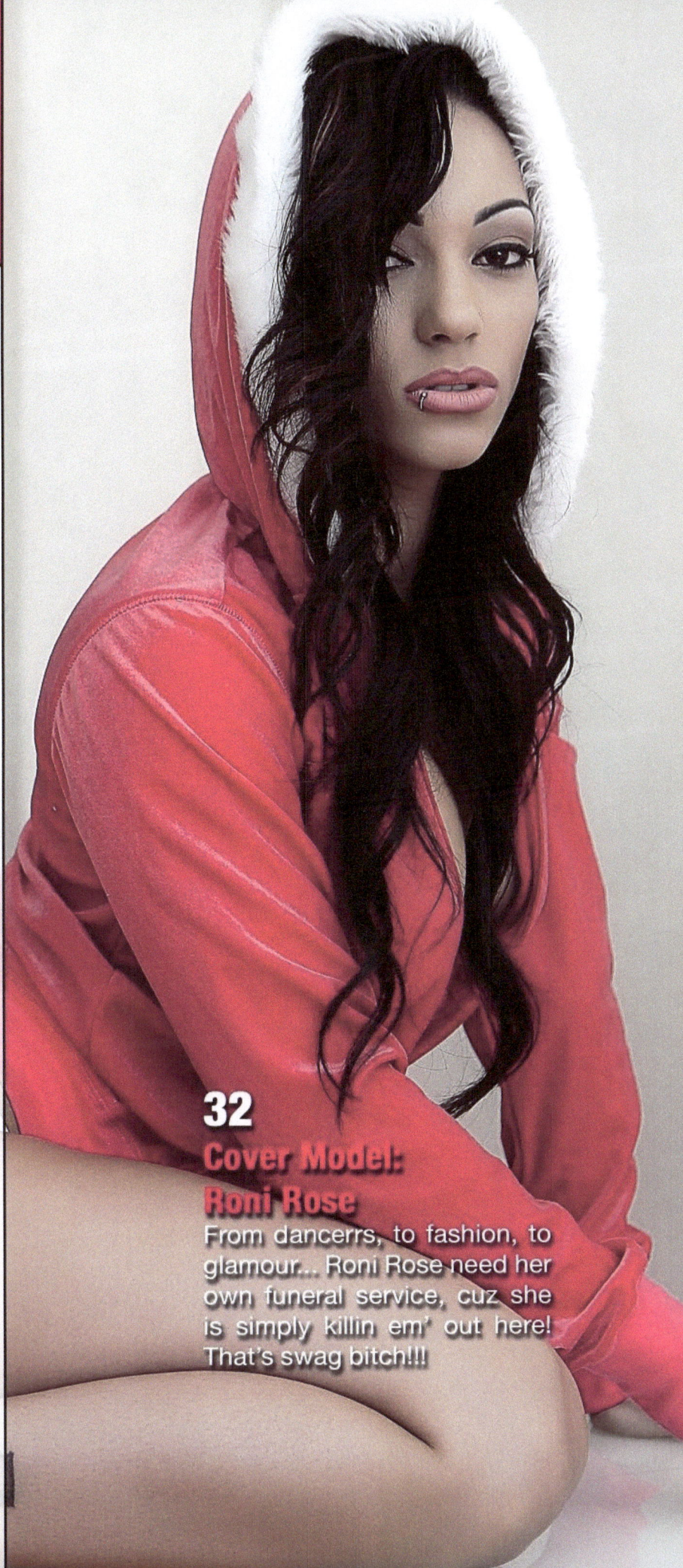

Features

08
BANKSKY: The Legend of a Myth
You may have never seen him, but if you've seen his/her art, then you know the legend.

09
From Street Hustler to Hollywood Icon: Idris Elba
Move over Denzel, there's a new sheriff in town.

10
A Gentleman's Guide to Breaking Up
Delicate times call for delicate meausres.

12
Tiger Lily
If beautiful curves get your engine going, then welcome to overdrive.

16
Total Fucking Bad Ass: Tom Hardy
It's hard out there for a tough guy, but Hardy has no problem keeping up.

17
Young Simba: J. Cole
In a land of mindless fools with recording studios, the rap artist with a message is King.

18
Amber Beautiful
I love dark chocolate. I love it even more when its covering a nice pair of curves like these.

22
After Obama: A Legacy in Review
The changing of the guard is almost upon us. So what of our latest White House leader. How did he do?

26
Fox Candy Girl of the Month: Mimi Toribio
When you have a banger like Mimi in the room, don't make any sudden moves. This girl is dynamite! Nobody move, nobody gets hurts!

38
Lala West
We don't usually encourage bringing sand to the beach, but in the case of this Trinidadian hottie. We simply couldn't resist bringing the beach to the sand.

42
Bella Nykole
Bella is just anohter pure example of everything that's absolutely awesome coming out of Atlanta right now.

32
Cover Model: Roni Rose
From dancerrs, to fashion, to glamour... Roni Rose need her own funeral service, cuz she is simply killin em' out here! That's swag bitch!!!

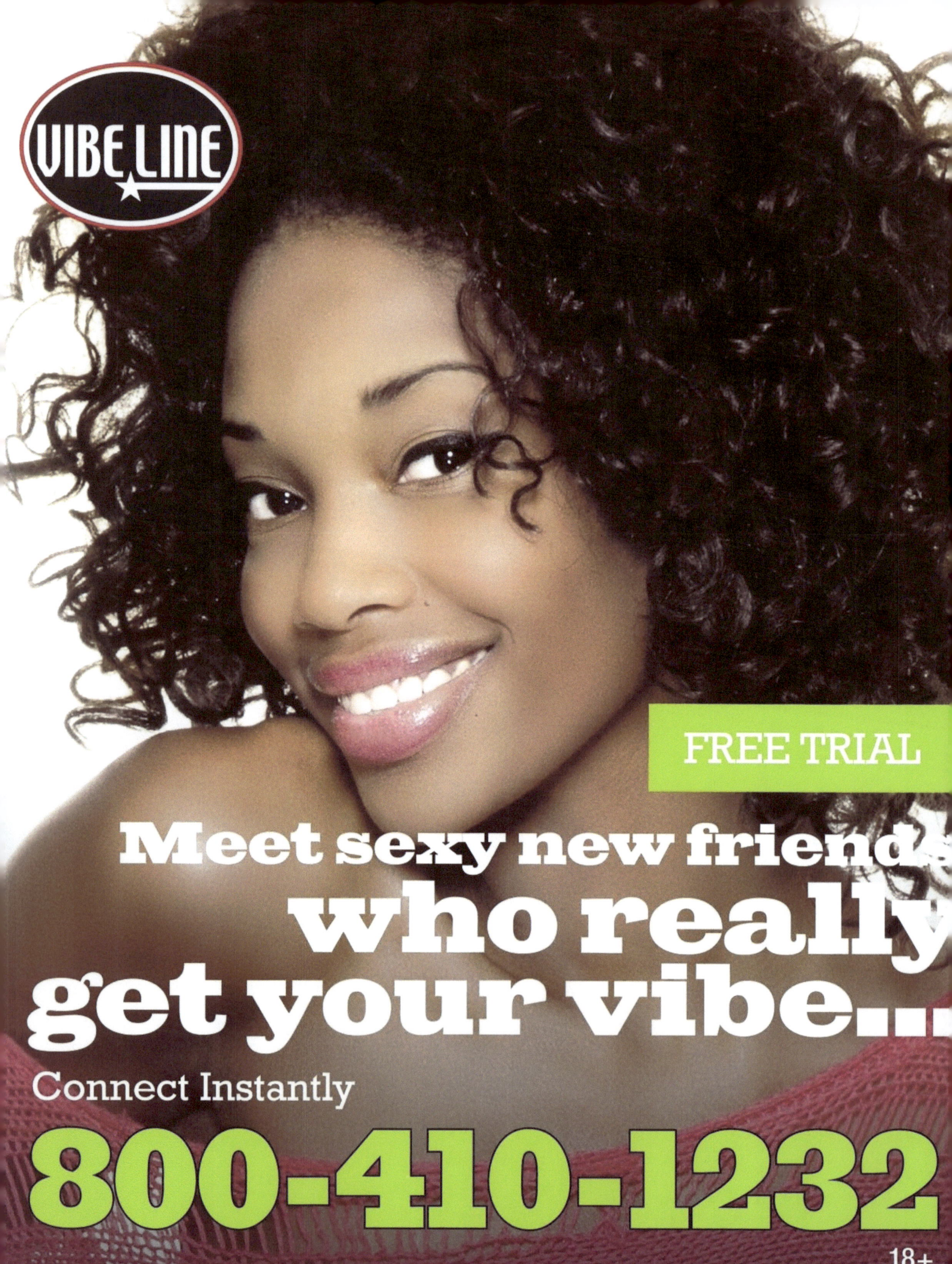

Editor's Letter

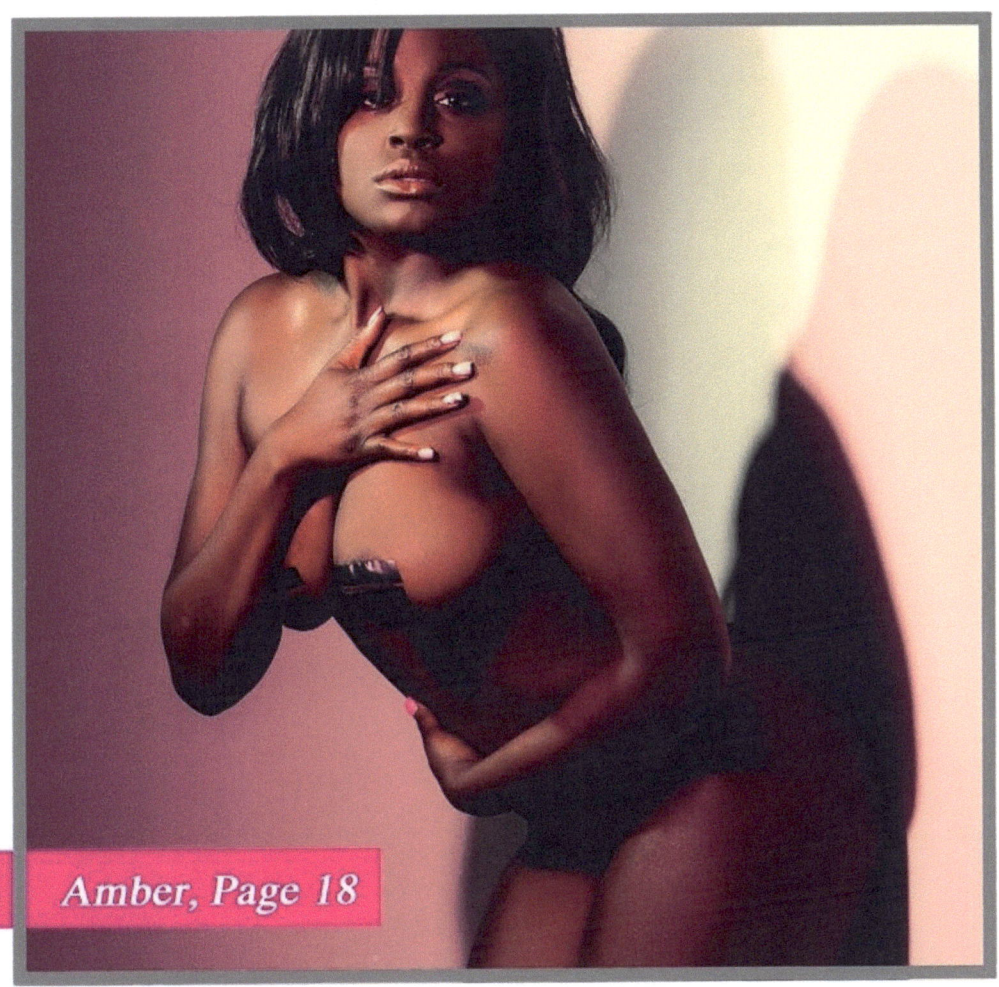

Amber, Page 18

If you keeping up with Foxtail Magazine (instead of the Kardashian), then you know FTM is the fastest growing underground, urban glamour magazine on the Internet. You also know that we issue one of the hottest magazine with delectable models, intriguing articles, and much more. Believe me when I say, we absolutely have no intention of stopping. We don't like to brag, so just come in and see for yourself. Just to up the ante... we went all around the country looking for delicious divas. Our search took us from N.Y. to California, and back again!

Down in Gerogia, we discovered the impeccable beauty of Bella Nykole. Then we shot down to Mississippi, and scooped up a little Trinidian beauty, LaLa West. Fellas yes, the ass is amazing! Bouncing back to Chicago, we had a chance to get up with chocolate drop, Amber MadBeautiful. If you haven't had the pleasure, I encourage you to do so! After Chicago, we flew out to New York and got a little Fox Candy, Mimi Toribio. Mimi is a Jawbreaker that will cripple your sweet tooth. Last, but certainly not least. We headed out to sunny California, and landed in the San Francisco Bay, and was graced with our cover girl: Roni Rose. Bruh...

In this issue, we review the legacy of our President: Mr. Barack Obama. We also give you a little advice on how to break up like a gentleman. This is issue is jam-packed with features on J. Cole, Idris Elba, Tom Harkdy, and Bansky. This is Foxtail. Enjoy!

Charles C. Rigby II
Editor-In-Chief

Join Foxtail Magazine's many followers at www.instagram.com/foxtailmagazine

WIN $50! #iluvfoxtailmagazine

Take a pic of your favourite page in the issue, tag it #iluvfoxtailmagazine on Instagram, Twitter or Facebook. One person, selected at random, will win $50.

WE'RE GOING IN FOR THE KILL!

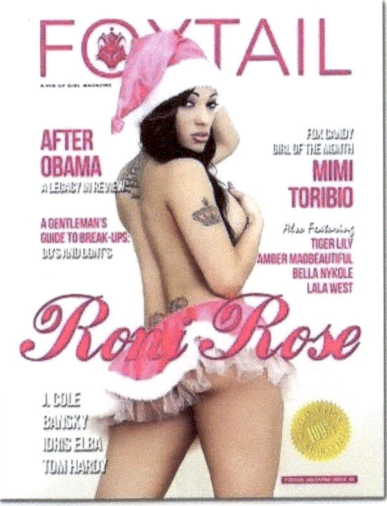

ISS. #5
NAUGTHY & NICE EDITION

The Locker Room

CELEBRITY QUOTABLE *By Clara Freeman*

Celebrities can be as cold as a November wind chill when they feel the need to "read" or clarify "shade" from a fellow celebrity. Here are some recent memorable and even notable "Celebrity Quotables" for your reading enjoyment:

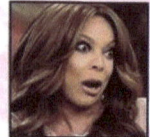

"There's nothing wrong with online dating, you just have to vet out the killer."

Wendy Williams talking it up with her co-hosts (audience).

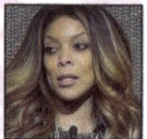

"Khloe, you are a white woman. Know your place!"

Wendy Williams's responds to Khloe Kardashain, after she posted pictures of herself, Kim and Kourtney, on Instagram, with the caption *"The only KKK to let Black men in."*

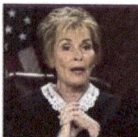

"I don't watch Reality TV. Most are train wrecks."

Judge Judy doesn't mince words. She expressed her views on a recent **Wendy Williams** show when asked about recent drama on a Reality TV show.

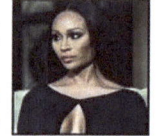

"Being friends with NeNe is a fulltime job. More draining than my fibroids could ever be."

Cynthia Bailey of the Real Housewives of Atlanta, giving **RHOA** face time on her friendship with **NeNe Leakes**.

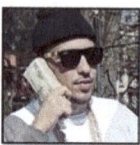

"I don't feel like love needs publicity."

Rapper French Montana, talking to **Wendy Williams** about his relationship with **Khloe Kardashian**. Critics had insinuated that the rapper was an opportunist.

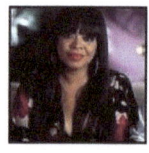

"It's hard being a broke celebrity."

Singer Shanice Wilson, promoting her show, alluded to their years of being broke and the shame of having to file for bankruptcy.

FOXTAIL MAGAZINE ALBUM OF THE MONTH
J. Cole | 2014 Forest Hills Drive

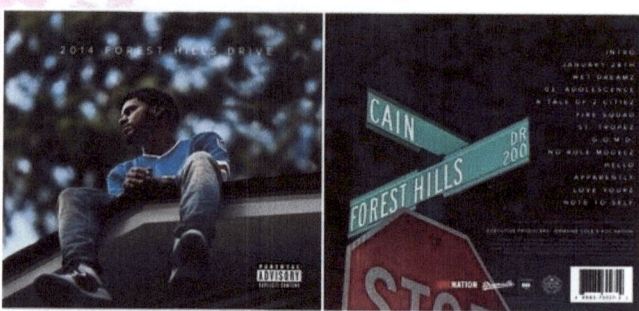

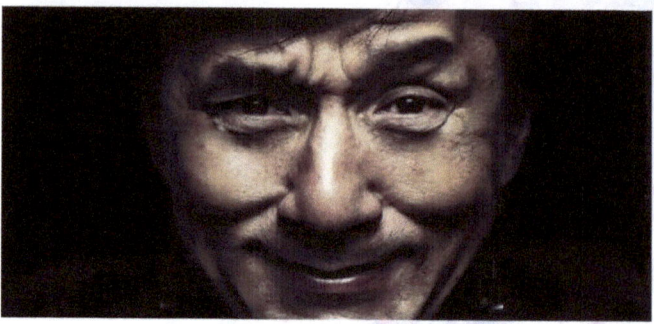

CELEBRITY FUN FACTS: JACKIE CHAN
By Christopher A. Smith

Jackie Chan has regaled the world with a lengthy career as one of the top martial arts actors. His blend of powerful Kung Fu along with a very keen comedic style makes him memorable. Chan makes it a point with his films to show just how involved – and how dangerous the fighting in his films are. Even to the point of showing just how he got to have a permanent hole in his head as a result of his stunts.

The shocking situation took place while filming the opening sequence of Armor Of God in 1986. The scene called for Jackie to jump from a wall to a tree branch in close proximity to it. The first take went well, but Chan wanted to do another. He jumped and made it, but the broke. Jackie wound up falling fifteen feet, striking his head on a rock which led to him seriously fracturing his skull to the point that a piece of bone entered his brain. He was flown to the nearest hospital and endured an eight-hour long surgery. Here's the miraculous part: the very next day he was not only alert, but walking around comfortably!

Jackie would have a lasting reminder of the injury – the hole in his head is sealed permanently with a plastic plug along with hearing loss. Talk about suffering for your craft.

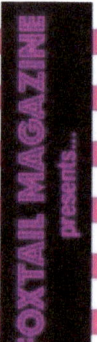

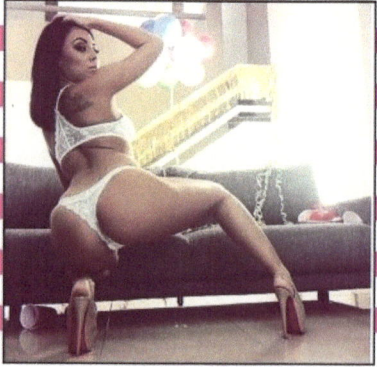

@officialgianna
Gianna Nicole; 1.2M+ Followers

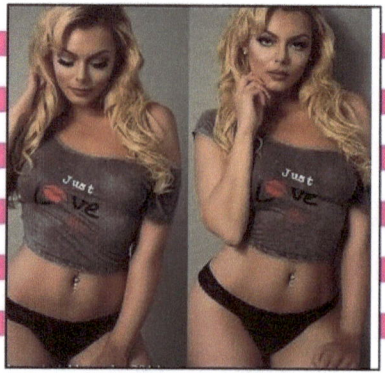

@victoryasecret
Victorya Ashley; 14K+ Followers

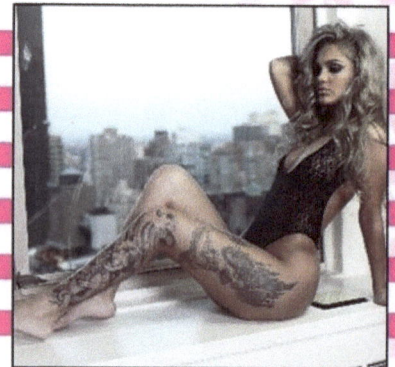

@amina.blue
Amina Blue; 17K+ Followers

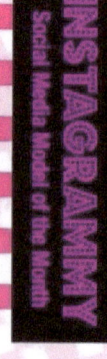

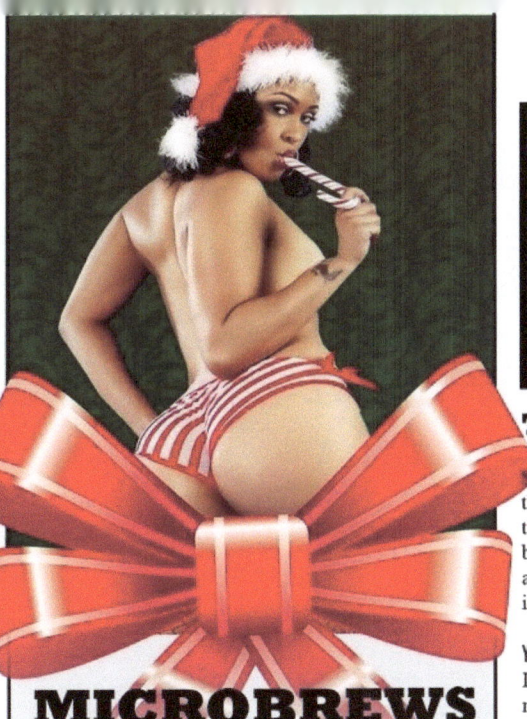

MICROBREWS THAT MAKE 'TIS THE SEASON

BY CHRISTOPHER SMITH

Sixpoint Autumnation
Sixpoint Brewery, Red Hook, Brooklyn New York
Average Price: $6.00

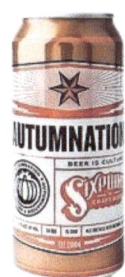

This seasonal choice from Sixpoint is robust but not too harsh on the palate and bears a nice flavor throughout. It's mostly available on draft so be on the lookout.

Peppercorn Saison
3 Stars Brewing Company, Washington D.C.
Average Price: $5 – 7.00

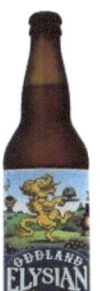

The District's first microbrewery has planted a flag for excellence with this offering, It's a year-round beer but perfect for the season with its delicate citrus and a full body of spice that reveals itself in the first few sips.

Ommegang Adoration
Ommegang Brewery, Cooperstown, New York
Average Price: $9.00

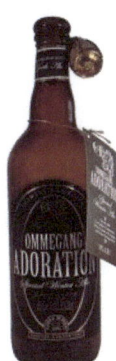

This winter offering from the highly acclaimed Belgian brewery is bold for a couple of reasons. First, it's ABV is at 10, which is hefty for your holiday cheer. The dark malt taste is balanced out well by the slight hopping and a combo of spices including cardamom & orange peel.

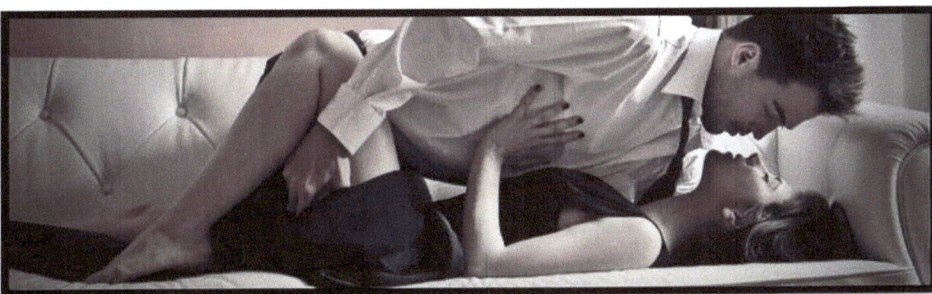

Top 5 Reasons Why Sex After 30 is Just Better

Sex used to be thought of as a young man's game, that idea was perpetrated by the fact that the younger you are the more virile you are. Times have changed and men are taking care of themselves better than ever making everything from one head to the other work at a higher level. There is truth in the saying that sex is like pizza (when it's bad it's still good) but the fact is that sex in your twenties and before is just putting a peg in a hole over and over again with no real rhyme or reason. By the time you reach your thirties you have picked up a few tricks and sex is just plain better for more than a few reasons.

YOU KNOW WHERE IT'S COMING FROM
If you are in your thirties you are probably either married or in a long term relationship; even if you're not you most likely have at least one booty on speed dial. Men may joke about not getting laid very often in a long term relationship, but if that is the case they are doing it wrong. It is great to know where your sex is coming from both in the sense of knowing you are going to get some and knowing that that some you get isn't coming with a Valtrex prescription.

YOU KNOW A LOT MORE
By your thirties you know what you like and you don't like; you also probably know a lot more about how to use what god gave you. You know more positions and you know that being a generous lover usually benefits you in the long run. You have also figured out by this point how to communicate in bed so you get what you want without seeming creepy or insecure.

YOUR PARTNER KNOWS A LOT MORE
Unless you are robbing the cradle (we won't judge) it is a good bet that your partner will know a few tricks of her own. She forgot about Cosmo a long time ago and just learned from experience what drives men wild. By her thirties she probably knows what she is into as well which may suck if she's not into what you're into but will be awesome if she is.

INHIBITIONS ARE LOWER
This may be a little contradictory but sex after thirty is actually a little more adventurous. Yes you and your partner know what you like and what you dislike but you also know that what you like can get a little repetitive and boring sometimes. I don't have any hard data but I would venture to guess that the demographic for those purchasing a Kama Sutra is above the age of thirty; and how awesome does that sound? Just pray that you are just as flexible as you were in your twenties.

YOU ARE STILL RELATIVELY YOUNG
Think about it; you get all of the benefits of being more mature but your body is just a few years removed from its twenties. This means that you have the energy to go all night and the strength to pull off some of those standing moves that are in the Kama Sutra that you just bought. Sex is awesome at any age but just like a fine wine it gets better with age. Just remember that when it comes to great sex quality is always better than quantity.

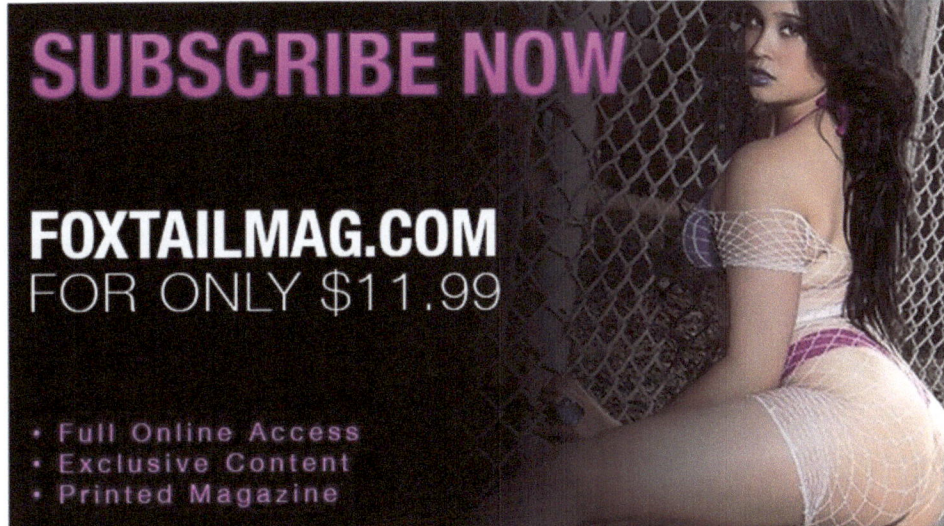

BANKSY
The Legend of a Myth

By Arthur Thares

The first thing that you need to know about Banksy is that no one knows anything about Banksy; seriously, the CIA could take a few pointers from this guy. There have been many hoaxes claiming to have revealed the identity (or identities) of Banksy, but nothing has ever been substantiated. This prolific street artist has rose to fame first because of his socio-political street art and second for his ability to stay unexposed in a world of social media and a 24 hour news cycle. The man – if it is a man – is something of a legend among street artists and those that appreciate the art alike. If you do know who Banksy is then you already know just how interesting this character is, if you have never heard of him before then you are about to learn about one of the most interesting and enigmatic human beings to ever (or never) exist.

The definition of Banksy's career all hinges on who you ask. Some would call him an artist plain and simple while others, like Michael Bloomberg, still choose to call him a vandal. No matter what you call him, Banksy is undeniably creative and thought provoking. Though Banksy as a person is still as unknown as he was when he first started out his persona has only grown through the years. He started as a free hand graffiti artist but did not rise to fame until he switched to stencil art; something that he attributes to a chance encounter with garbage while hiding from the cops.

His rise to fame has been one filled with nothing short of intrigue. He came up with other street artists who were known collectively as "The DryBreadz Crew," but soon gained his own individual fame with his art which is heavily political with the bite of humor and satire. If his art wasn't enough he has also played some pretty amazing stunts like setting up a kiosk in New York and selling Bansky originals for 60 bucks a pop or the wildly underappreciated film Exit Through the Gift Shop. Street art has made Banksy famous but selling original pieces from highly publicized art exhibitions has made him rich. If Banksy truly is one man - with an incredible gift - he is estimated to be worth around 20 Million USD; not too shabby for a guy who runs around coloring on the sides of buildings. Though all of his wealth comes from art in one form or another Bansky is obviously a great business mind too; the artist has started his own film production company as well has self-publishing many popular photo books including the best seller Wall and Piece.

Banksy has laid pretty low in 2014 and it is anyone's guess as to why. It would be easy to speculate that he was arrested, or died, or maybe just ran out of creativity, but a better bet is just that the busy artist needed some down time or is planning something really big. No matter what the reason behind his rather sudden and elongated departure from the public eye it is safe to say that we have not seen the end of Bansky or his mysterious and interesting street art.

FROM NIGHTCLUB HUSTLER TO HOLLYWOOD ICON

By Berber Ormeling

The sky rocketing career of Hollywood's favorite male actor, Idris Elba (42), proves that the American dream is also possible for an English fellow. After breaking through in the UK as an actor in 1995 as a gigolo in the hit series Absolutely Fabulous, Idris decided he wanted more and in 1998 he moved to the States in search of the American dream. Idris was eager to become famous and felt England was too small for him and he wanted more. He had also always felt very familiar with the country and its identity, especially through its hip-hop music.

The money that he received from the sale of his UK house only lasted him for a year though and after that year he still saw himself forced to sell weed at the door of a well known New York club, where he worked as a porter. Occasionally, he returned to the UK to do some acting gigs to get by but Idris swore not give up on his acting dream. Not even when his pregnant wife left him and he had to live in his van for two months. Idris kept the faith though and eventually snapped up the role of Stringer Bell on HBO's hit series The Wire in 2002, which became the jump-start for a successful career as a famous Hollywood actor.

Idrissa Akuna Elba, born 6 September 1972, first grew up in multicultural Hackney in East London. His father, Winston, escaped poverty in Sierra Leone and immigrated to the UK with his wife Eve in search of a better life. Elba's father eventually found a job at the Ford factory and his mother Eve, originally from Ghana, found work as a typist. When Idris was 14 he started helping his uncle out as a wedding DJ and he also started up his own DJ company with some friends. At 16 Idris left school to enroll in the National Youth Music Theatre, thanks to a £1,500 Prince's Trust grant. Soon after, he joined the Music Theatre. Here, he sang for the first time publicly, and he instantly got hooked on the thrill of being on stage. But work was hard to come by in the next years and for a while the biggest part he could achieve was the one of suspect in a BBC Crimewatch Drama where he had to chop up his girlfriend.

In between roles, Idris took on whatever work he could from tire fitting to cold call advertising to pay the rent. There was the occasional modeling job though and in 1992 he also started his professional career as a London DJ under the name DJ Big Driis. It's not until he made his move to the USA, that his acting career finally took off big time. After years of struggle in 2002 Idris finally became instantly famous for his role as drug gangster Russell "Stringer" Bell in the hit series the Wire.

An American dream finally came true when Idris was asked to play the lead role of his lifetime in the movie 'Walk to freedom'. The movie was released in 2013 and Idris received his first Golden Globe nomination for his role as Mandela. Now, Idris Elba just may became the next James Bond. He would also be the first Black actor to ever play the role. That is if he gets the job.

12 Things You Don't Know About Idris Elba

• He first tried talking with an American accent when he auditioned for a role at the Wire but in the end dropped it and still got a part.

• In preparation for his role as Nelson Mandela he spent a whole night in a cell of 8ft by 7ft on Robben Island. Idris could not sleep the entire night because he heard strange sounds and he is convinced the former jail is haunted.

• Idris had a girlfriend named Judith of 19 when he was only 14 and pretended to have a job instead of being in school just for her, which became very difficult one day when she caught him doing his homework.

• He practiced his American accent at his regular barber's shop in Flatbush.

• Idris would love to make a musical one day.

• Shortened his first name Idrissa to Idris as class mates used to tease him all the time for having such a feminine first name.

• He actually would love to play the first black James Bond ever.

• Idris Elba gets sexually aroused by bow ties.

• His guilty karaoke secret is Bob Marley's 'One Love'.

• In 2012 he made a Channel 4 documentary called Idris Elba's How clubbing changed the world, in which he interviewed the likes of Will.I.am, Paul Oakenfold and David Guetta.

• Idris Elba was named Essence's annual 2013 Sexiest Man of the Year.

• He has been a fan of Arsenal FC since he was a teenager, but only has seen 2 real matchs.

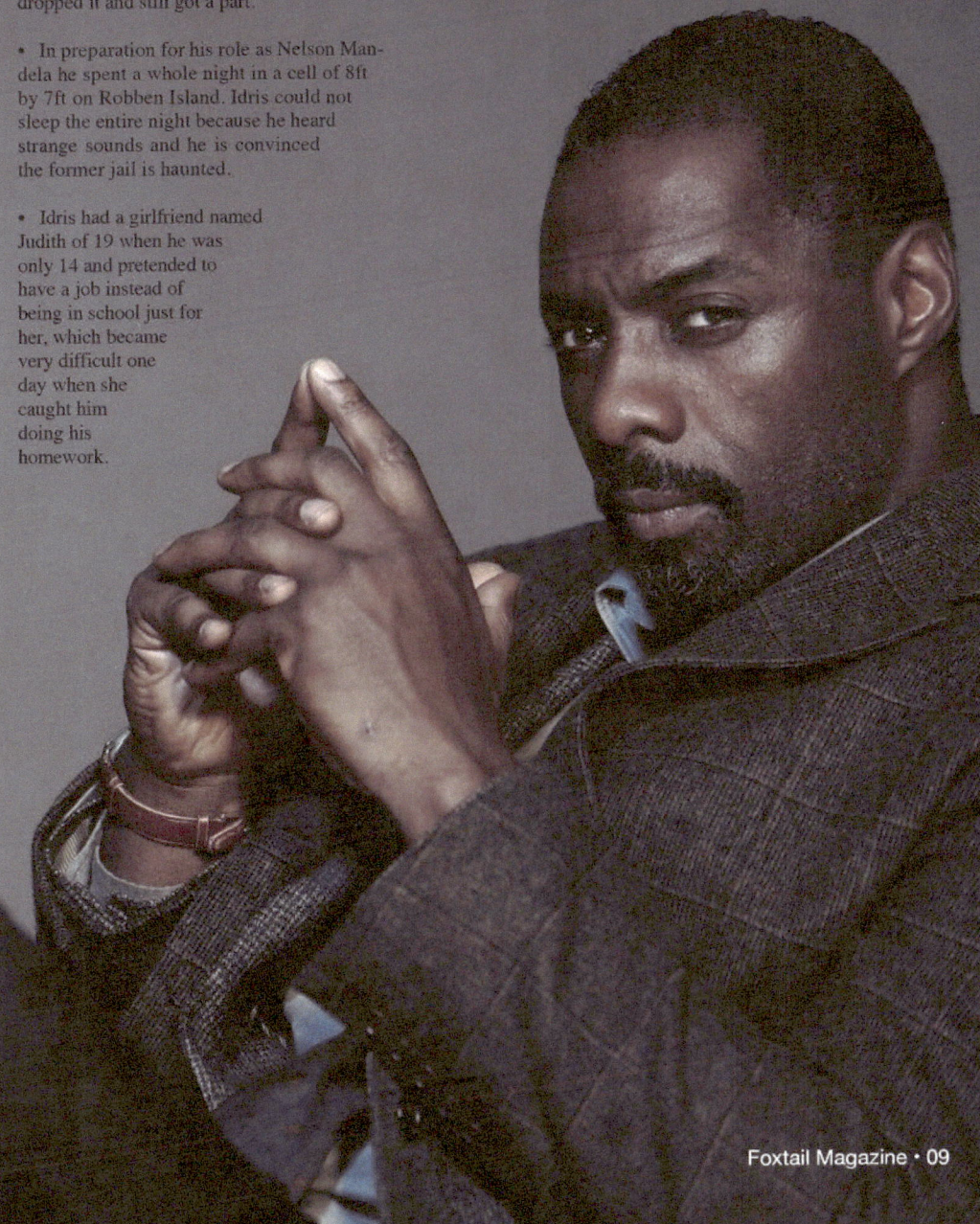

A Gentleman's Guide to Breaking Up: The Do's and the Don'ts

By Viola Irvin

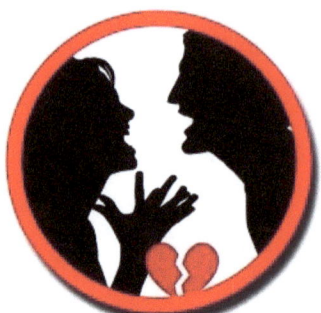

RULE #1:
OVER IS OVER

When a relationship is over, it's over. *DON'T* prolong the inevitable by getting her to dump you or cling to the hope something will change. Remember, you are breaking up for a reason. Dragging thing along will only make the end hurt more for the both of you.

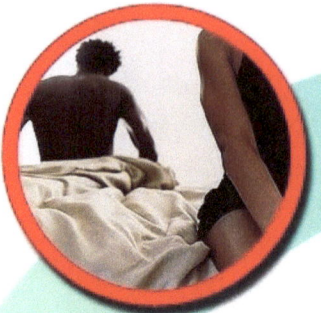

RULE #2:
TAKING A BREAK IS B.S.

DON'T take a temporary 'break.' It's a lame excuse that means, "I don't love you anymore, but fear being alone forever." Getting back together after 'the break' might rejuvenate your relationship at first, but the habits of the old will return, leaving one or both parties dissatisfied again.

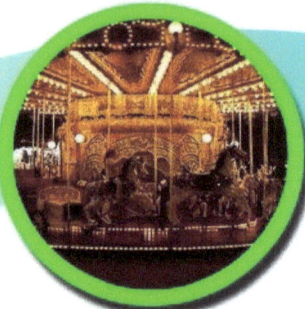

RULE #3:
NO MERRY-GO-ROUND

DO avoid entering into an on-again, off-again relationship situation, because eventually it will be off permanently and who knows how much time will be wasted clinging to the hope the problems from the first break-up will disappear.

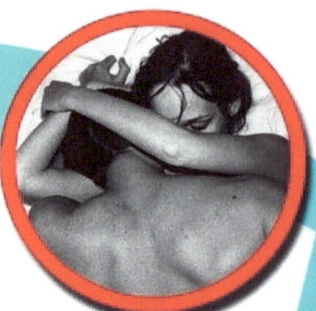

RULE #4:
BREAK UP SEX IS A BAD IDEA

As tempting as it is *DON'T* engage in break-up sex. It only complicates matters and doesn't allow for a quick, clean break. A break-up needs to be final. Finality gives both parties closure. One more ride on the saddle will cause chafing.

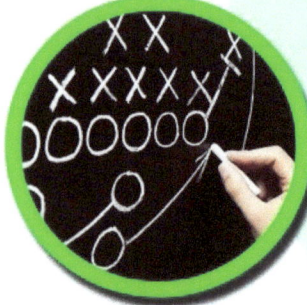

RULE #9:
NOTHING WRONG WITH A GAME PLAN

DO plan ahead what you are going to say. You don't have to follow a script word for word, but having a clear idea of what you will say makes it easier. Keep your prepared speech short. A long-winded explanation can be overwhelming and extra hurtful.

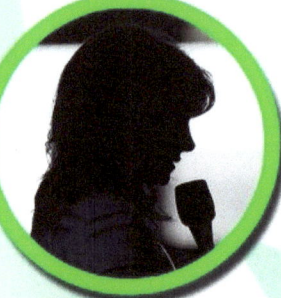

RULE #10:
LET HER SPEAK

After you nicely explained why you are ending it, *DO* let her speak and give her a chance to process. You might not like what she has to say. Women can be nasty about break ups. But, she still deserve her time to talk. This will all help ease heartbreak.

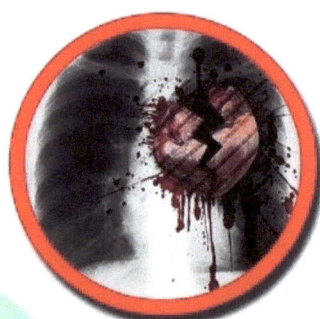

RULE #11:
FROM DUMPER TO DUMPEE

If you are the one that got dumped, just accept it and move on. *DON'T* try to win her back; it's too late. Besides, you don't have time to play that game. There are plenty of fish in the aquarium. Next time, instead of Tilpia go for the Lobster. Just beware of claws!

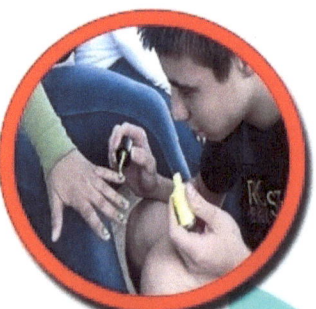

RULE #12:
AVOID THE "KISS OF DEATH" A.K.A. "THE FRIENDS ZONE"

Getting dumped should not serve as motivation. It's over, kid! As noble as it sounds, *DON'T* try to be friends. Reserve adding useless friends for Facebook. You didn't work as a couple; becoming friends will just be weird. A clean-cut break is always the best route. No contact. No Instagram pic liking. No nothing.

It doesn't matter if you have been married for 5 years or dating for 5 months, coming to terms with the realization that your wonderfully, perfect relationship is reaching an end is never an easy burden to bear. Having an amicable break-up makes the "Busting Your Car Window" situation less likely to occur. Sometimes, it might just be safe to stay in the relationship. On the other hand, if you really need to break up, then break up you must do. In the event of a break, we have your back. Just follow these simple do's and don't to breaking up, and you just might ease through the breaking up blues without a scratch. You could possible save yourself a fortune on auto window replacements.

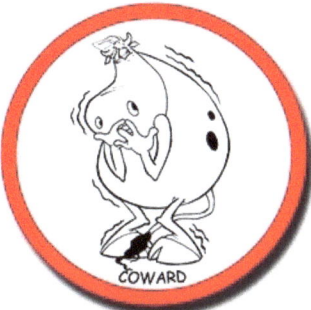

RULE #5:
TEXTING IS COWARDICE

This should go without saying... *DON'T* end your relationship via text or social media. Be a man! If you can't tell her to her face, you probably shouldn't be breaking up in the first place. A text just mean you don't have a clear cut reason for breaking up, or it just means you're a coward.

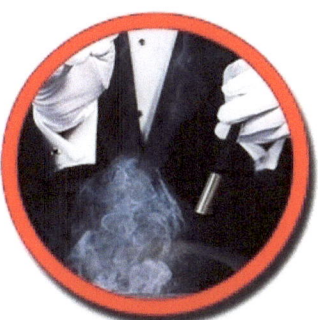

RULE #6:
DISAPPEARING ACT ARE FOR MAGICIANS

DON'T just disappear, even if you never were truly serious. If you've been on more than 3 dates, that is the start of a relationship, albeit a casual one. Not responding to her texts or calls is cruel and cowardly. Every relationship even it's only been a few short months or weeks deserves an official "Sorry, I'm not that into you" conversation.

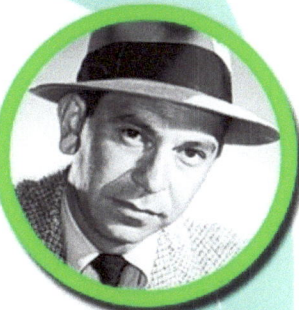

RULE #7
JUST THE FACTS, MAN

Honesty is still the best policy. *DO* be direct and honest without being hurtful. You know why the relationship isn't working and it's necessary to verbalize that reason clearly. Beating around the bushe will only lead to an adverse outcome.

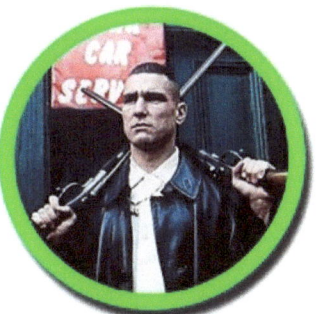

RULE #8:
LOCK AND LOAD

Tears might come, she might beg, but *DO* stick to your guns. You wanted to end the relationship and her tears should not change the fact.

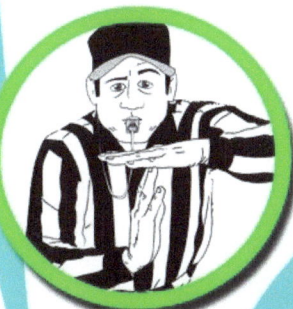

RULE #13:
TAKE A BREAK

DO take a break from the dating scene for a minute. Moving on doesn't mean hoping into bed with the first pair of tits and ass you see at the club. There's nothing wrong with a rebound to get back into the swing of things, but getting dumped is not an excuse for a sexual orgy.

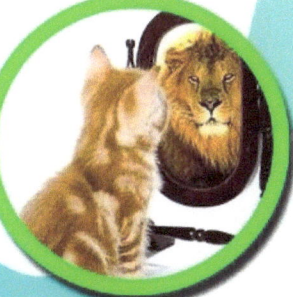

RULE #14:
GET TO KNOW YOU

DO treat yourself like a rock star. Believe is or not, breaking up is a traumatic experience. Take some time to reflect on how thing went wrong, and how to improve next time. Stay positive and remind yourself of why you're awesome.

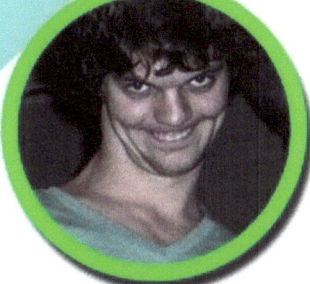

RULE #15:
DON'T BE A MR. CREEPY, NO STALKING

DO delete your ex from your social media presence. You don't need to read her twitter updates or stalk photos of her at the nightclub. There's nothing wrost than obsessing over pictures of your replacement.

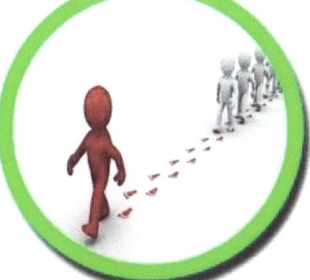

RULE #16:
OUT WITH THE OLD, IN WITH THE NEW

DO start fresh with your next girlfriend. The most imperative thing is don't let this failed relationship negatively affect future relationships. Relationships and people are different. No two are ever alike. Always start a new relationship with a clean slate, and a clear head.

TIGER LILY

INSTAGRAM • @CHANDA2087

PHOTOS BY • FOSTER PHOTOGRPAHY

Height • 5'4" | Weight • 150 | Hair Color • Black | Eye Color • Brown | Measurements • 36B - 29 - 40

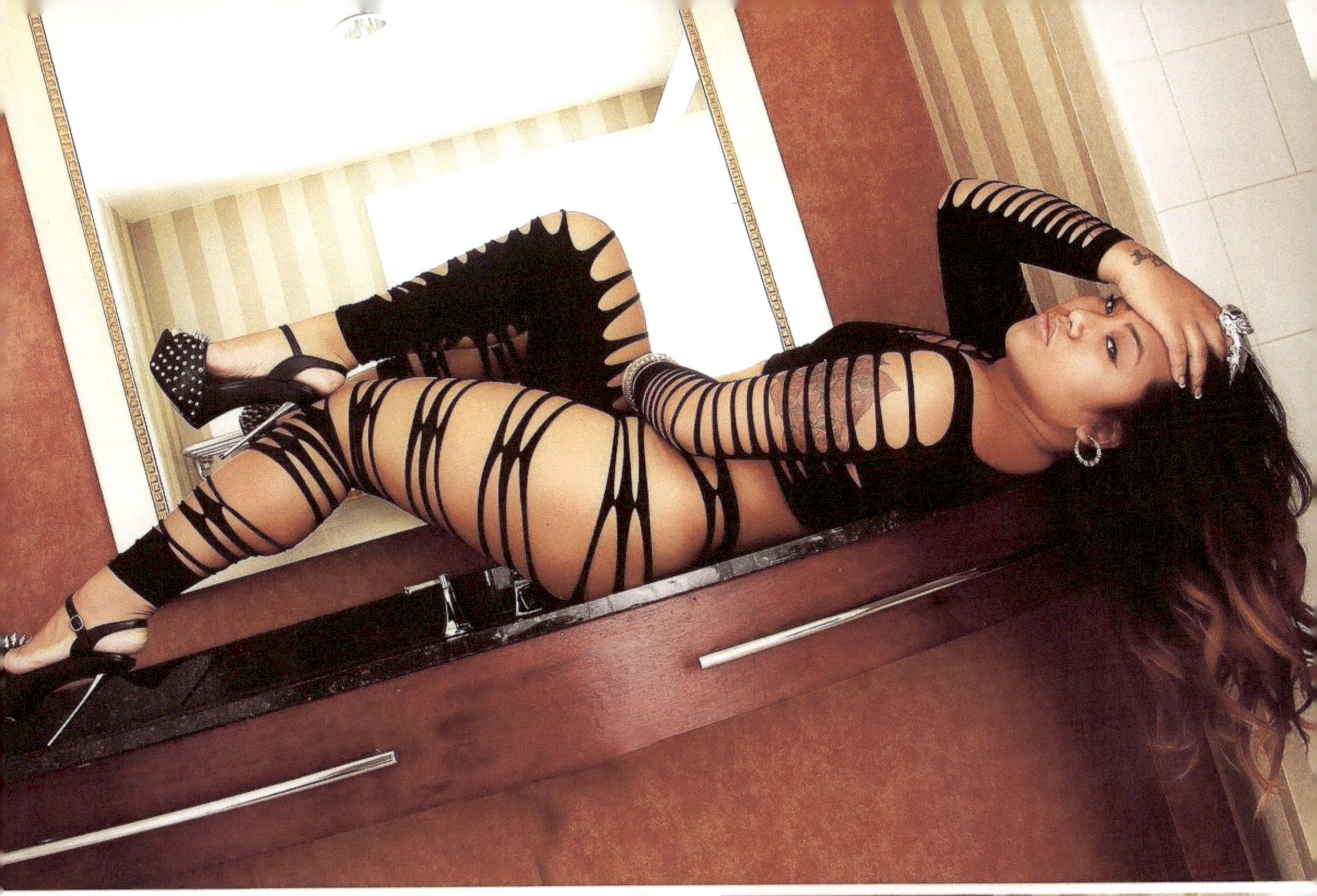

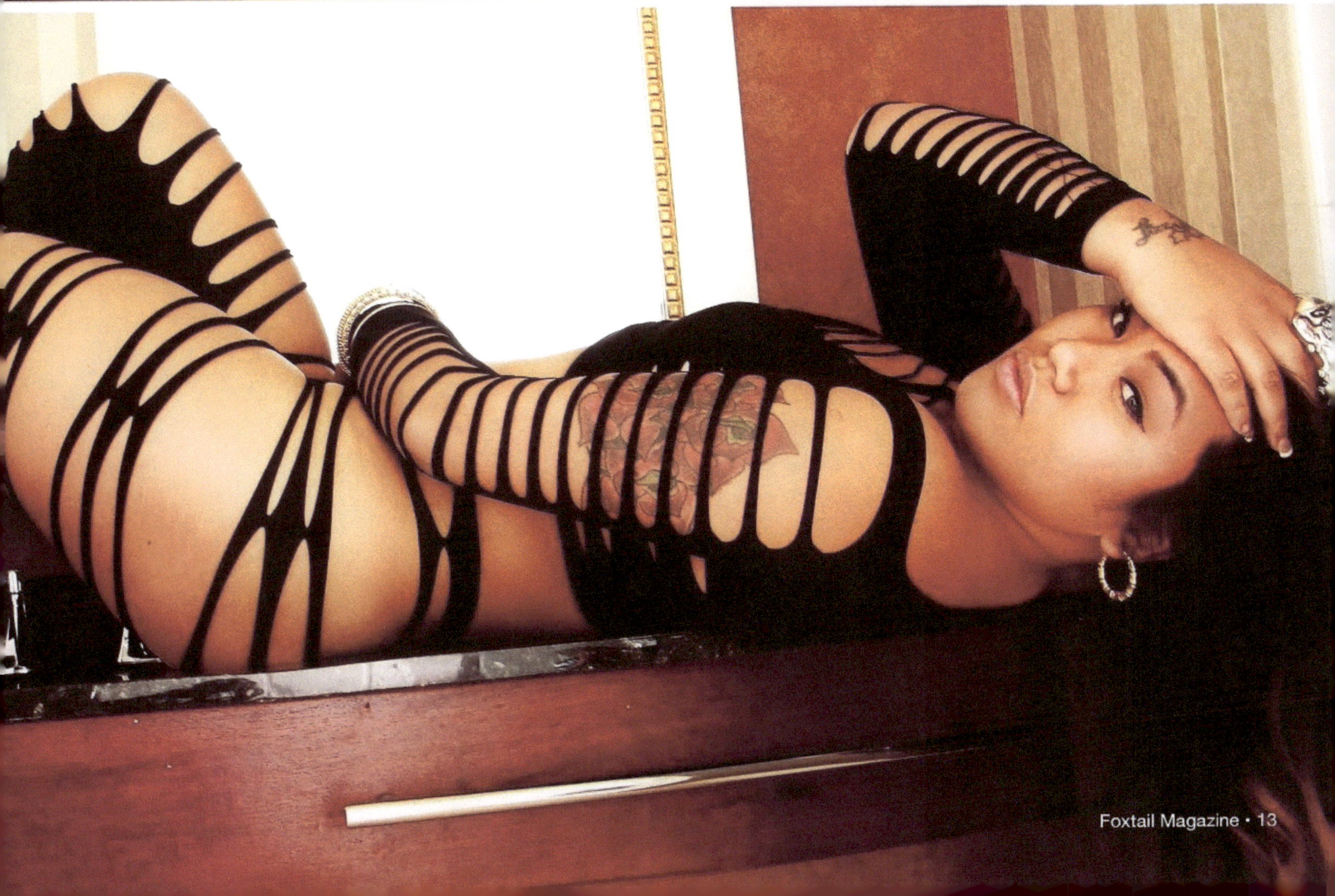

Foxtail Magazine • 13

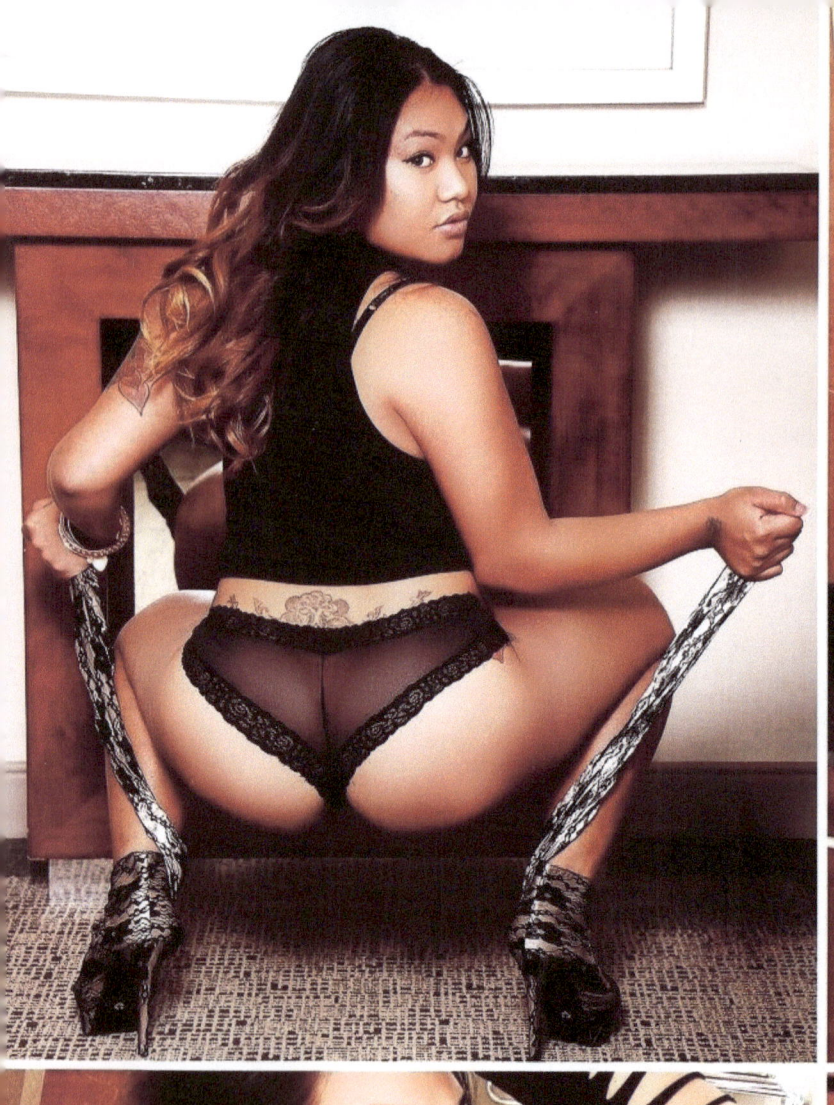
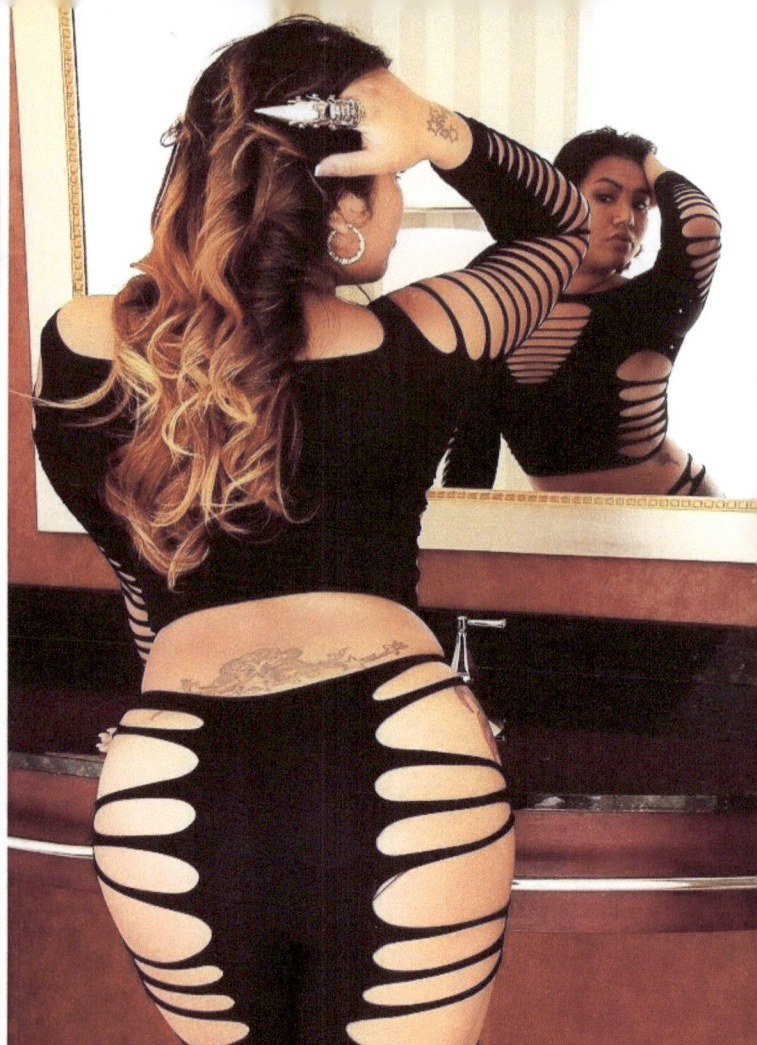
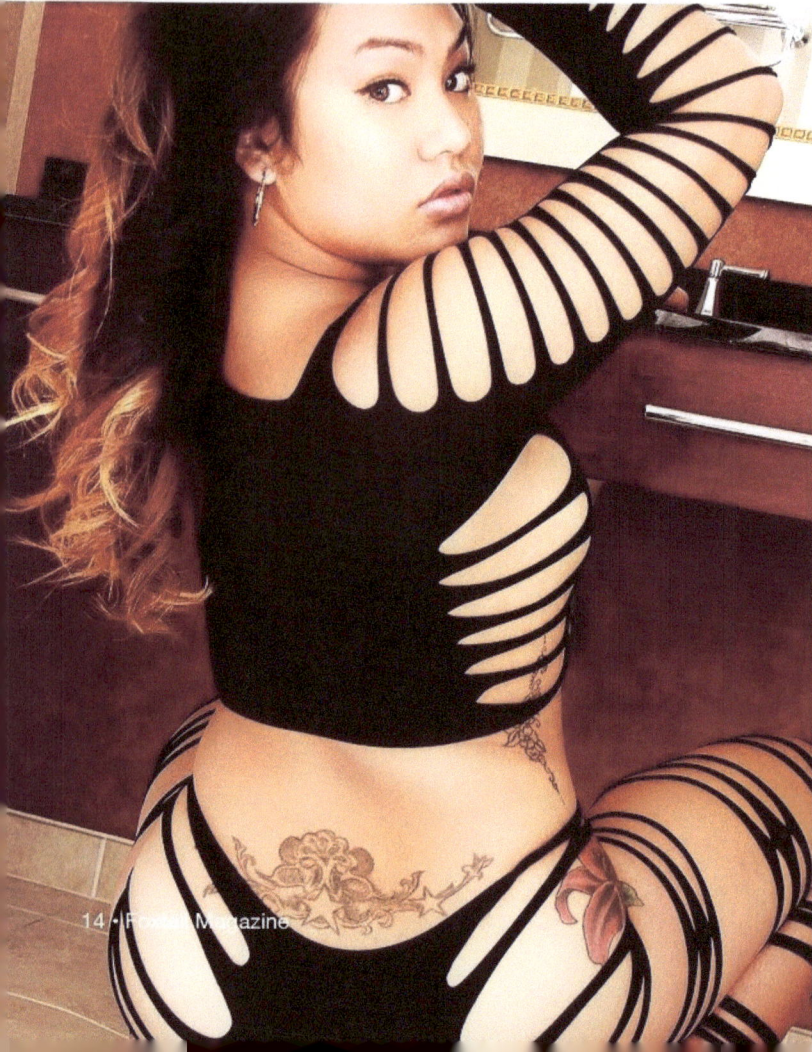
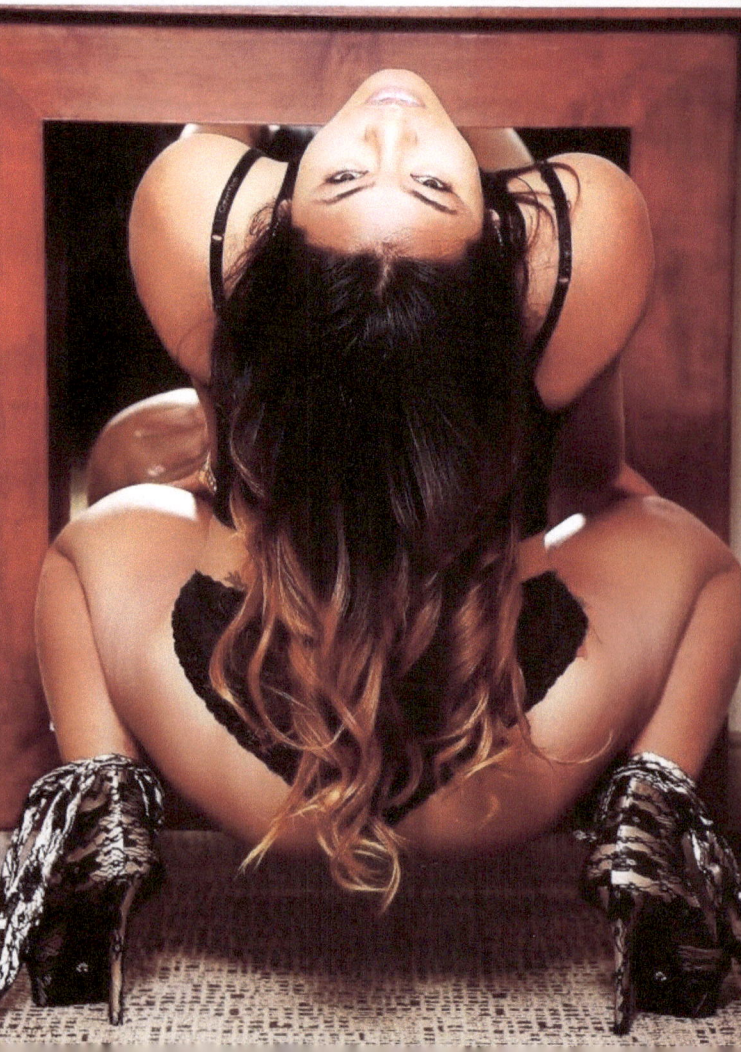

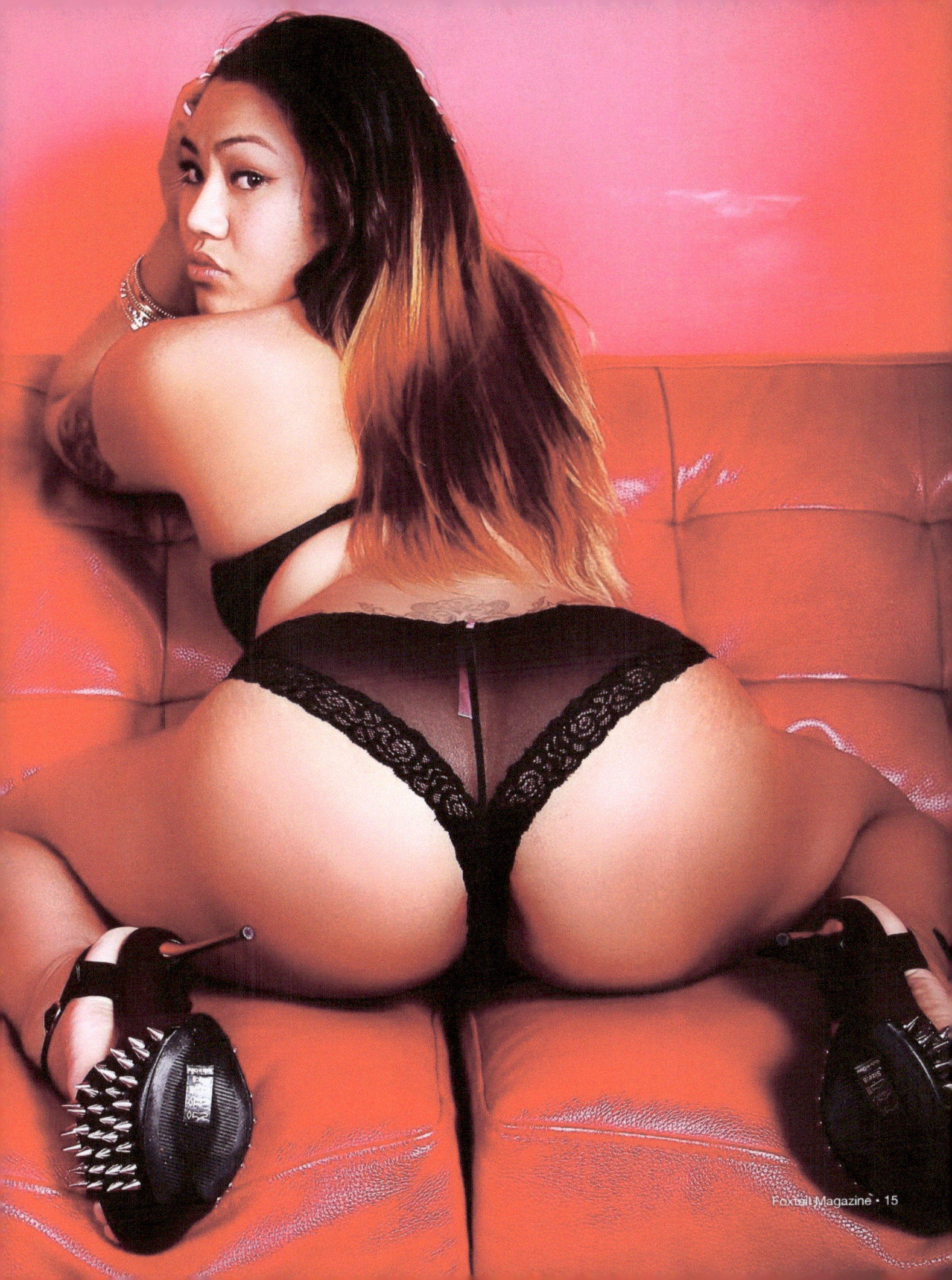

TOM HARDY
TOTAL FUCKING BAD ASS

Most would know him as the man who broke Batman's back and reeked general havoc on Gotham City, but the man behind Bane's mask is even more interesting than the character he portrayed. Though his star is just beginning to rise Hardy has been an impressive character actor for some time and has been in some of the most interesting indie films you have never seen along with being "that one guy" in many popular films.

My first experience seeing Hardy on film was the Independent movie "Bronson" for which he won a British Independent Film Award for best actor. The award was well deserved as Hardy perfectly portrayed one of England's most violent inmates of all time. Not only was Hardy's acting incredible but he went above and beyond by being full frontal naked for half of the movie. Aside from porn stars and Michael Fassbender there are not many dudes out there bad ass enough to do something like that. As long as man parts don't make you squeamish I would definitely recommend watching this film.

Though Bronson was possibly his best performance to date he is probably better known for his more mainstream appearances. He first caught attention for his role in Band of Brothers and a subsequent turn in Black Hawk Down. He also got a little attention for portraying the villain in 2002's Star Trek: Nemesis. From there his notoriety only grew as he stole scenes in Guy Ritchie's RocknRolla as well as Christopher Nolan's Inception, but it wasn't until his turn as the muscle bound Bane in The Dark Night Rises that he became a household name.

Though the movies have all been markedly different one attribute of his characters is always the same; he is a total fucking badass.

This may be his on screen persona but it is fueled by the fact that Hardy is a badass in real life and the kind of guy that men want to be and women want to be with. Hardy's handsome face, chiseled body, and oozing charisma both on and off screen were hard earned by a life that could only be described as eventful so far.

Hardy was not always a badass and had a pretty normal childhood being raised by a novelist and humorist father and an artist mother. He studied at multiple private schools (which he got kicked out of) and two different drama schools finishing at the Drama Centre in London. At 21 he was awarded a modeling contract with the Models One agency, but it did not last long.

In his teens and early twenties Hardy battled drug and alcohol problems which led to delinquent behavior and started his road to the badass hall of fame. Hardy married young but the marriage didn't last, an event he blames on his substance abuse. After his marriage fell apart Hardy fathered a son named Louis by a girlfriend. That relationship did not last but Hardy gave love a chance one more time marrying his now wife in July of 2014.

Even with all of the temptations of Hollywood it seems as though Hardy's demons are behind him and he has rose from the ashes to become one of the most badass men in Hollywood. He has multiple projects coming up but we really want to see him in more movies where he beats the shit out of people, preferably in the title role.

By Arthur Thares

12 THINGS YOU DIDN'T KNOW ABOUT TOM HARDY

1. Has the name of his agent, Lindy King, tattooed on his arm because he promised the he would get her named tattooed on him if she got him into Hollywood.

2. Hardy agreed to fight David "The Haymaker" Haye in a celebrity boxing match for charity, but it has yet to take place.

3. He put on 42 pounds of muscle for Bronson by doing 2,500 push ups a day.

4. Arrested for stealing a car and gun possession but didn't see time because his accomplice was the son of a British diplomat.

5. Nominated for 14 awards and won two.

6. On top of being a badass actor he has also penned two television series which have been sold to production companies and owns his own production company that is set to produce its first movie in 2014.

7. His role in Bronson inspired Steven Ogg's character Trevor Phillips in Grand Theft Auto 5.

8. Largely regards Gary Oldman as the best actor ever and has had the opportunity to work with him in three different movies.

9. Good friends with Sherlock star and fellow Star Trek villain Benedict Cumberbatch.

10. Did his own stunts for Black Hawk Down and was even set on fire.

11. Has a borderline phobia of wigs stating once in an interview, "I don't like wigs the way some people don't like clowns." He's so bad ass he still dawns them any time the role requires it of him.

12. Based his character, Forrest Bondurant, in Lawless on the cartoon grandmother in the Tweety and Sylvester cartoons.

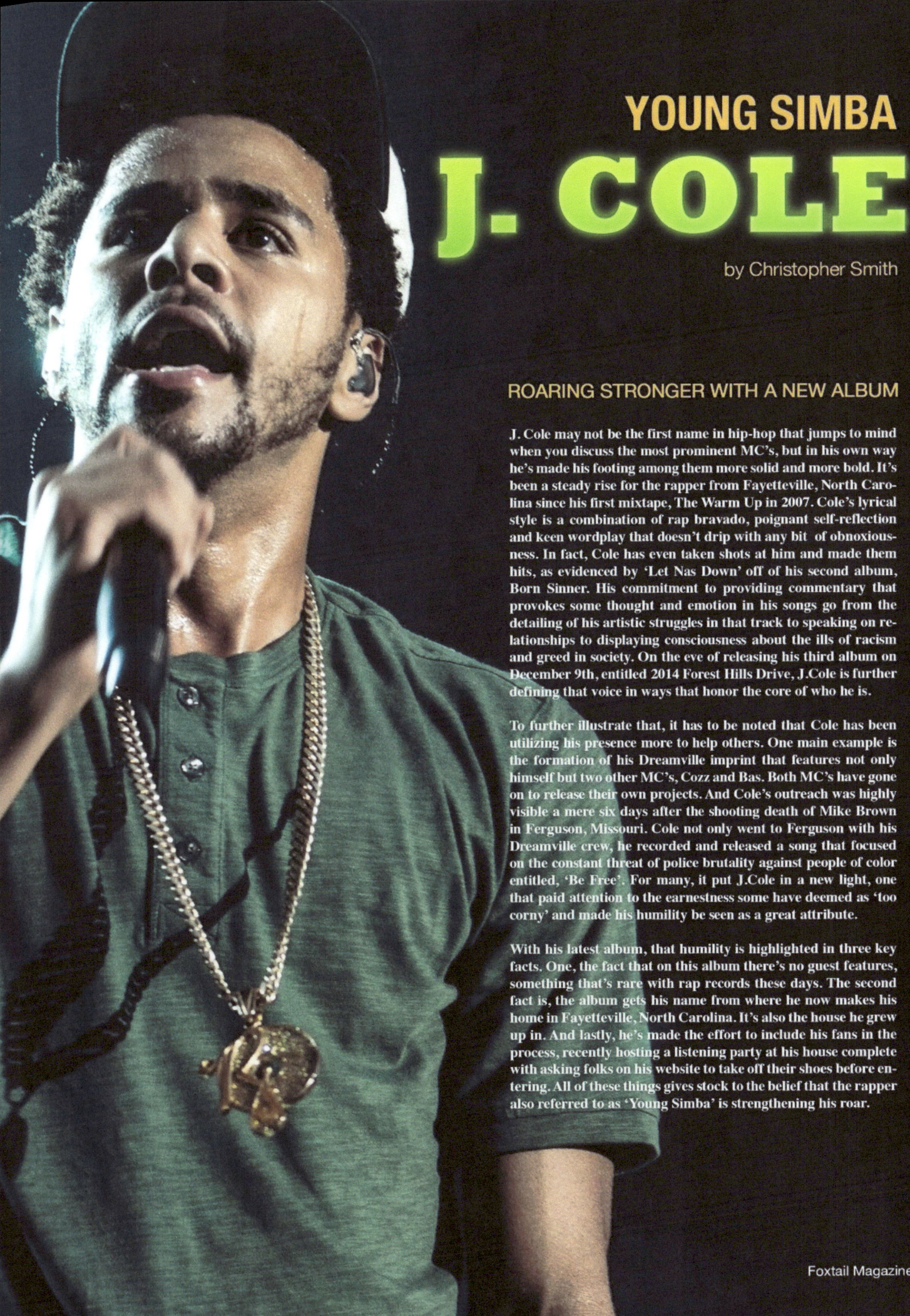

YOUNG SIMBA
J. COLE

by Christopher Smith

ROARING STRONGER WITH A NEW ALBUM

J. Cole may not be the first name in hip-hop that jumps to mind when you discuss the most prominent MC's, but in his own way he's made his footing among them more solid and more bold. It's been a steady rise for the rapper from Fayetteville, North Carolina since his first mixtape, The Warm Up in 2007. Cole's lyrical style is a combination of rap bravado, poignant self-reflection and keen wordplay that doesn't drip with any bit of obnoxiousness. In fact, Cole has even taken shots at him and made them hits, as evidenced by 'Let Nas Down' off of his second album, Born Sinner. His commitment to providing commentary that provokes some thought and emotion in his songs go from the detailing of his artistic struggles in that track to speaking on relationships to displaying consciousness about the ills of racism and greed in society. On the eve of releasing his third album on December 9th, entitled 2014 Forest Hills Drive, J.Cole is further defining that voice in ways that honor the core of who he is.

To further illustrate that, it has to be noted that Cole has been utilizing his presence more to help others. One main example is the formation of his Dreamville imprint that features not only himself but two other MC's, Cozz and Bas. Both MC's have gone on to release their own projects. And Cole's outreach was highly visible a mere six days after the shooting death of Mike Brown in Ferguson, Missouri. Cole not only went to Ferguson with his Dreamville crew, he recorded and released a song that focused on the constant threat of police brutality against people of color entitled, 'Be Free'. For many, it put J.Cole in a new light, one that paid attention to the earnestness some have deemed as 'too corny' and made his humility be seen as a great attribute.

With his latest album, that humility is highlighted in three key facts. One, the fact that on this album there's no guest features, something that's rare with rap records these days. The second fact is, the album gets his name from where he now makes his home in Fayetteville, North Carolina. It's also the house he grew up in. And lastly, he's made the effort to include his fans in the process, recently hosting a listening party at his house complete with asking folks on his website to take off their shoes before entering. All of these things gives stock to the belief that the rapper also referred to as 'Young Simba' is strengthening his roar.

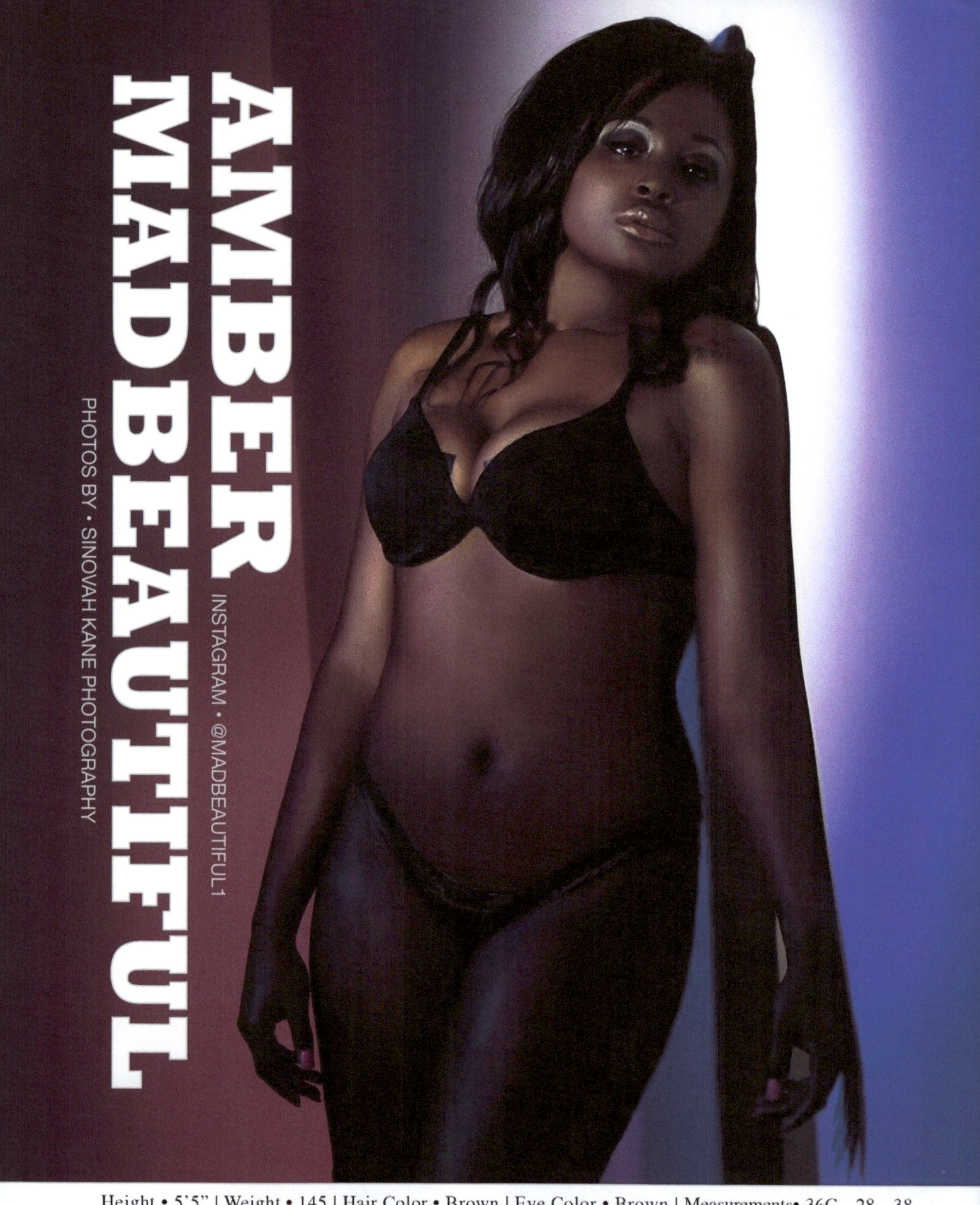

AMBER MADBEAUTIFUL

INSTAGRAM • @MADBEAUTIFUL1

PHOTOS BY • SINOVAH KANE PHOTOGRAPHY

Height • 5'5" | Weight • 145 | Hair Color • Brown | Eye Color • Brown | Measurements • 36C - 28 - 38

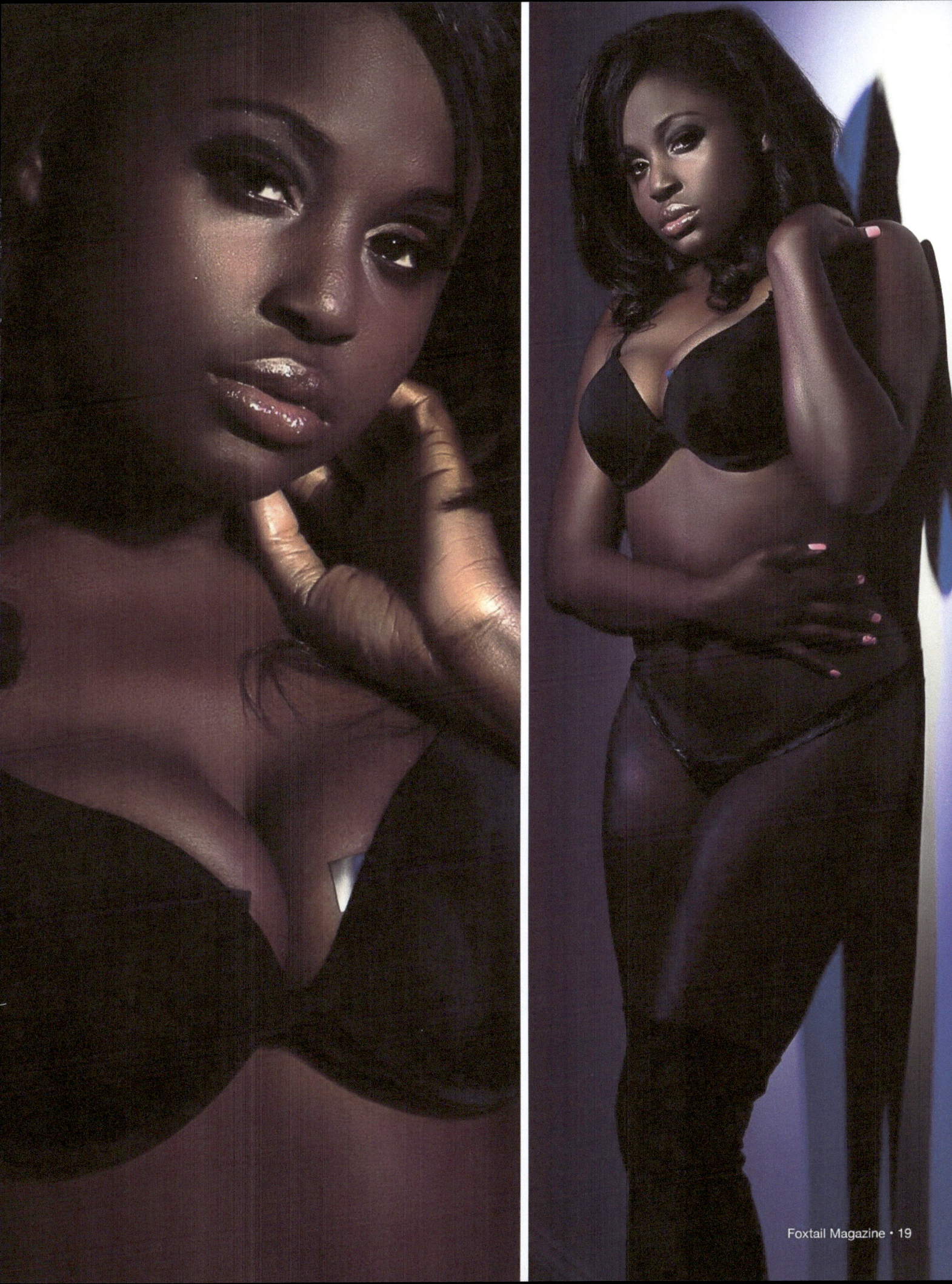

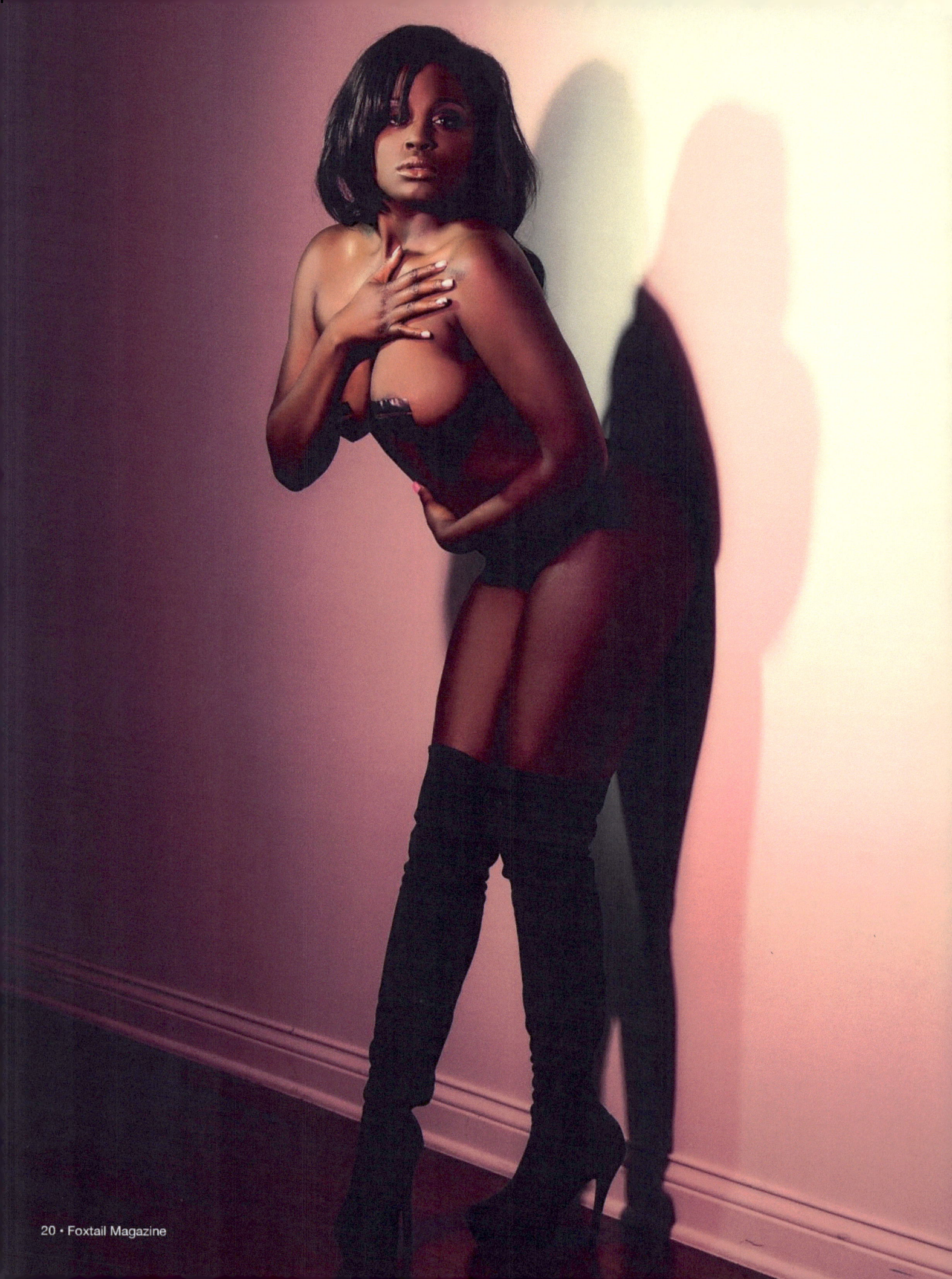

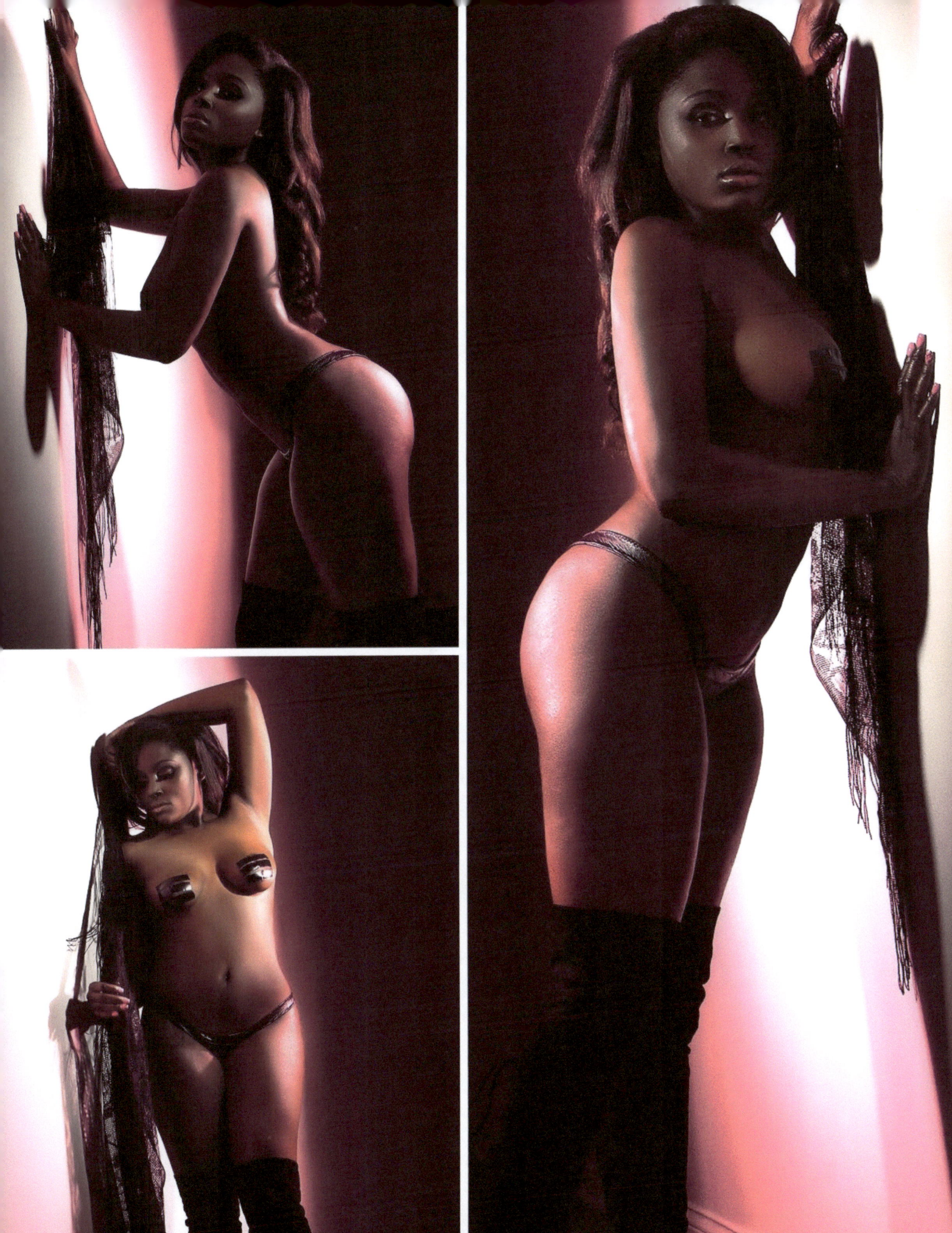

AMERICA AFTER OBAMA

By Josh Durso

A LEGACY IN REVIEW

Evaluating a Presidency comes with great challenges. Whether they're personal-political biases, or individual preference on various policy, or style, determining the quality of a President is a daunting task. Typically, it involves looking at the policies that the individual installed during their term, their ability to work with Congress and other branches of the government, and then evaluating the overall state of affairs when the individual leaves office.

President Barrack Obama was the first African American to hold the highest office in the United States, and campaigned on a promise of change – from the previous administrations ways. His racial background, policies, and positions made him an increasingly polarizing figure as the public got to know him better, and better. However, evaluating the legacy of a President – who also is one of the most polarizing figures in American history – comes with its own unique set of problems.

In fact, it isn't hard to classify President Obama as the most-polarizing President we've had in the last 30 years. That though, doesn't necessarily speak to his ability as a leader – but rather the state of divide that exists – depending on who you ask. It's important to acknowledge both sides, and understand that even the greatest of supporters – could not evaluate his Presidency honestly, and not admit that there were major opportunities for improvement. Similarly, those who have opposed the President, his views, and policies – can't evaluate his Presidency and say that he accomplished nothing.

One thing is certain – there has been no President of the United States in that time period who left the American people more divided than this sitting President has. His stance on social issues, the changes he made to the health system, and even his wavering stance on our presence in other countries. Whether you're talking about President Bush, or President Clinton – since the early 90s – there hasn't been a President that had a more divided following. President Bush was largely alienated – even by his own party – which left him with a less-impressive legacy than some of his counterparts, and President Clinton – even for all of his personal shortcomings and personal drama that found its way into the mainstream media – was still widely-known for his ability to work with a Congress that his own political party didn't even have control over.

As we close in though on the final two years of President Obama's second term as President of the United States, we can begin the process of evaluating his legacy. Applauding him for his accomplishments, understanding his opportunities and how we can right the ship moving forward into a new Presidency, and even begin understanding where he belongs in the setting of history.

What did President Obama accomplish while he was in the White House?

Defining what President Obama accomplished while holding office might be one of the most challenging questions to answer in a direct way. While those who support him will call on specific instances and call them victories – those who oppose him will likely use many of the same instances to validate their belief that he was one of the least-effective Presidents of all-time.

He came into office with the promise of "Change" and a campaign filled with all of the hope that the first-ever African American President would bring, and completely changed the way people handled a Presidential Election. It was the first "social" election, and as result – had some of the best turnout results of any election in the history of the United States.

Many though, have felt that halfway through his second term that his Presidency has been underwhelming. Even those from his own party have been left feeling as though President Obama hadn't followed through on enough of his promises to warrant the praise that has followed him. Looking at his track record – here is what stands currently as major accomplishments, or successes of his Presidency.

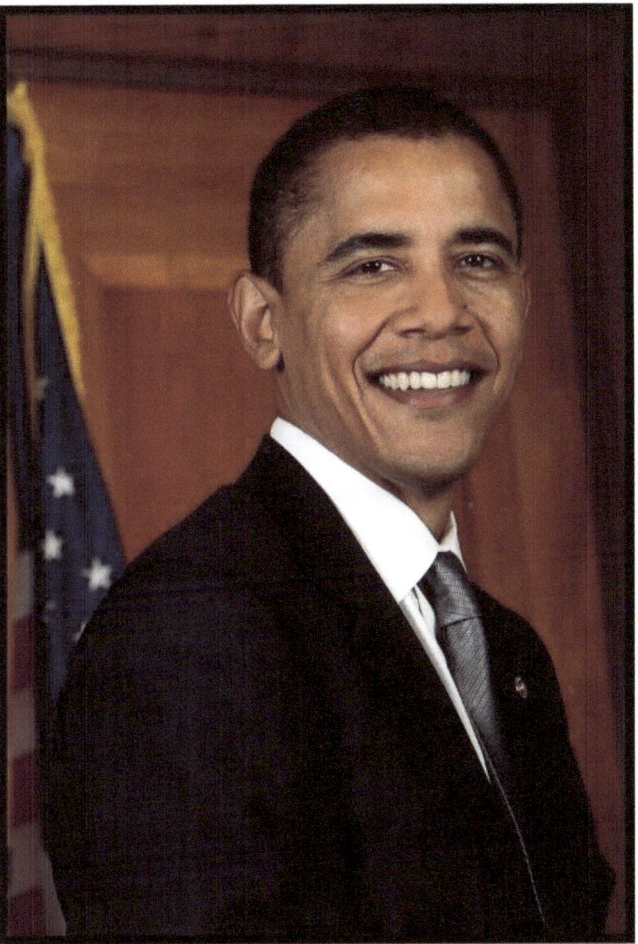

He ended the war in Iraq, and eliminated Osama Bin Laden. Debate as you may about his foreign policy, or his handling of Benghazi. At the end of the day, he ordered all U.S. military forces out of the country and they were effectively removed, and done with – in December of 2011. If that wasn't enough he ordered the raid that led to the killing of Osama Bin Laden in the same year.

He turned around the U.S. auto industry, and fixed the banks. GM and Chrysler received injections from the federal government to the tune of $62 billion – on top of the $13.4 billion in loans that the Bush administration granted to them – to ensure massive restructuring of the companies. Since the automotive industry hit rock bottom in 2009 – hundreds of thousands of jobs have been added in that respective industry. The banks that were struggling at the end of the Bush administration received recapitalization through a Treasury Department plan that got private money injected into the banking system – while creating a fund to buyout "toxic" assets. The banks and automotive industry crashing would have resulted in catastrophic results.

He said 'goodbye' to "Don't Ask, Don't Tell." He formally introduced new policy that gave gays and lesbians the opportunity to serve openly in the military.

He signed the Affordable Car Act in 2010. There are going to be people who vehemently disagree that this was a positive thing to come out of his administration – but the truth is that the health care reform that has happened under President Obama is far more than had been passed or done, correctly or incorrectly, since the introduction of federal programs after the Great Depression. Roughly 32 million Americans who were previously uninsured would have the opportunity to be insured with his program.

He signed a $787 billion stimulus package that made everything thereafter possible. Say what you want about his policies, but if it weren't for that stimulus package that was called the American Recovery and Reinvestment Act in 2009 – nothing else would have mattered because the economy was heading toward completely collapse. The private sector has had 57 consecutive months of job growth, and has added a total of 10.9 million jobs in that time period.

He reformed Wall Street. He signed the Dodd-Frank Wall Street Reform and Consumer Protection Act in 2010 which ensured that the financial sector saw re-regulation and a change to the policies that ultimately brought on the recession of the first decade of the new-century. It even created the Consumer Financial Protection Bureau which exists to keep banks and lenders in line.

He's actively been promoting and working on marriage equality. He is the first President of the United States in some number of years to actually take marriage equality seriously. Many states have implemented changes in legislation since his taking office – largely in part due to his fight for the cause.

He's made climate change a priority. Even with immense challenge from his opposition he launched the profitable clean-energy revolution. He also remained a steady-opposing force to the proposed Keystone XL Pipeline.

He cut taxes on the poor and middle class while reducing the deficit. He raised taxes on the wealthy, and reduced the tax burden on those who made less. While that wasn't the most-popular move he made as President – it can't be argued that it helped a great deal of people in the process. He also was a part of reducing the deficit by 50% during his tenure in the White House.

That being said, there are always two-sides to every story. Even for all of those accomplishments while in office – there will be many who see his Presidency as a compete-and-utter failure. This comes with the territory though of holding the highest office in the land.

Where did President Obama fail during his tenure in the White House?

Every President has missed opportunities, or shortcomings. There are both pros and cons to every presidency and to call it any other way would be a travesty. That being said, there are many who believe the President failed pretty badly when it came to his terms in office – and we're still just halfway through his second-term.

Perhaps one of the most unique aspects of President Obama's tenure as leader of the United States is that while those who believe he has done miraculous things for the country have arguments that are very statistically driven, citing figures, numbers, and polling results to support what he has done.

On the other hand though, those who believe President Obama's tenure in office has been a failure have mostly-subjective – but entirely legitimate gripes with the way President Obama has executed and carried himself during his Presidency. That's not to say that facts and statistical analysis aren't present in their criticisms of the President, but rather the issues they have with him as a leader are generally viewed as obvious issues, that don't need statistical analysis to prove.

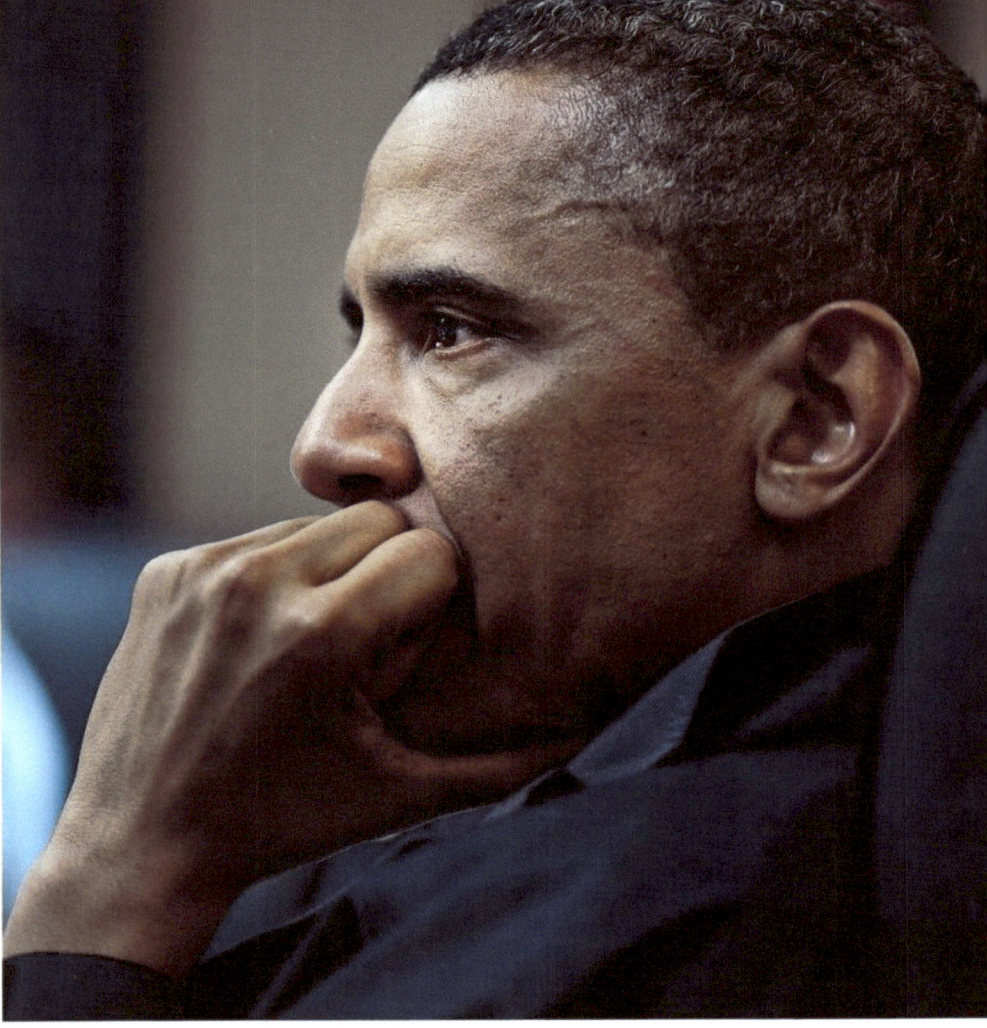

Racial divide in the United States is worse now under President Obama. According to a Bloomberg Politics Poll, it shows that racial divide – and racial tensions are at all-time highs. For President Obama – the first African American President who promised and campaigned on the premise of "Change," screams utter failure. The poll shows that 53% of Americans believe that race relations have gotten worse under President Obama. And this isn't a poll of exclusively African Americans – this is a universal poll – and the same poll even found that 11% more white respondents said race relations have gotten worse than black respondents.

He took action on Immigration Reform that his opposition say is a violation of his rights. It was universally understood that President Obama was going to take executive action on immigration after gridlock in Congress that was largely blamed on Congressional Republicans. However, even a democratic majority couldn't make Immigration Reform happen – and now his opposition says that he has violated the Constitution.

The stimulus was a failure – even with the jobs gains that were seen in the months following. Many have argued that the stimulus that President Obama instituted didn't actually solve anything – and actually cost the U.S. money. A decline in labor force participation – which is the count of how many people are actually going out and working, or finding jobs – as well as growing personal debt per year. The deficit may have been reduced – but the lives of many actually got worse as time went on. There was also the issue of several billions of dollars in "shovel ready projects" that were later discovered to not actually exist.

Healthcare reform didn't actually reform – much less improve the healthcare system. The launch of Obamacare was one of the most talked about political moments during his administration. It was considered a pinnacle moment for his ability to follow through on one of the many promises he made when he took office, and even while he was campaigning. That launch was one of the most-botched, and most ineffective launches of its kind. It even cost the Health and Human Services Secretary Kathleen Sebelius her job back in April, thanks to the abysmal launch and execution of so-called healthcare reform. Even worse was the fact that it covered way fewer people than the Obama Administration claimed it would.

His foreign policy and handling of the continued terrorist threat is weak. Many believe that he prematurely pulled out of Iraq – even as warnings were coming in regarding the rise of groups like the Islamic State. Now, American lives have been lost at the hands of these extremist groups, and have been lost in gruesome videos documenting the beheading of western citizens. The Islamic State continues to grow – meanwhile the United States continues to flounder in their positioning – largely due to the lack of leadership from President Obama.

He has also disregarded Asian threats – as well as Russia. Russia and Ukraine had a rough 2014 together – President Obama never really took a significant stand, or drew a line in the sand regarding any of their actions. This is foreign policy, as well, but these are almost free-standing issues that stand on their own merit – separated from the umbrella of terrorism and the Middle East.

We can't forget about Guantanamo, the NSA, the VA, and more. All of these things have been either brushed under the rug, mismanaged, or a combination of both. President Obama wanted to separate himself from the actions of his predecessor – but really just talked a lot about those things – and even as the VA failed miserably – he didn't take a hard-stance on the issue until the situation was bubbling out of control.

He has a tendency to avoid taking responsibility, especially after the midterm elections. It was clear that the midterm elections were a failure, yet President Obama wouldn't take responsibility for the fact that Republicans won a larger House Majority, as well as winning a new majority in Senate, largely due to the displeasure with the job the President has done to date – especially in recent months.

What will President Obama's legacy look like in the end?

Ultimately, that is a matter of opinion. While it would be easy to say that President Obama has done well by looking at the numbers vaguely on the surface – a slightly different picture is painted when taking a closer look at the job he has done. He's experienced some of the lowest approval ratings in recent memory – and has lost a lot of trust from the general public due to his lack of leadership on key issues.

Perhaps though the most-defining aspect of his tenure in the White House will be his overall inability to lead on racial issues. While it's impossible to know now what his legacy will look like when he leaves office – it's really quite clear what his legacy will be now – even with the good he did for the country at the beginning portion of his tenure.

Even worse, he just might leave the White House and the United States in one of the most-divided states it has ever seen to date.

URBAN MARKETING • MUSIC MANAGEMENT • BOOKING AGNECY

I AM 3230

(708) 557-3230 • WWW.IAM3230.COM

FOX CANDY GIRL OF THE MONTH

MIMI TORIBIO

PHOTOS BY • MARTELL PHOTOGRAPHY

INSTAGRAM • @_mimiix3

Height • 5'5" | Weight • 145 | Hair Color • Brown | Eye Color • Brown | Measurements • 36C - 27 - 40

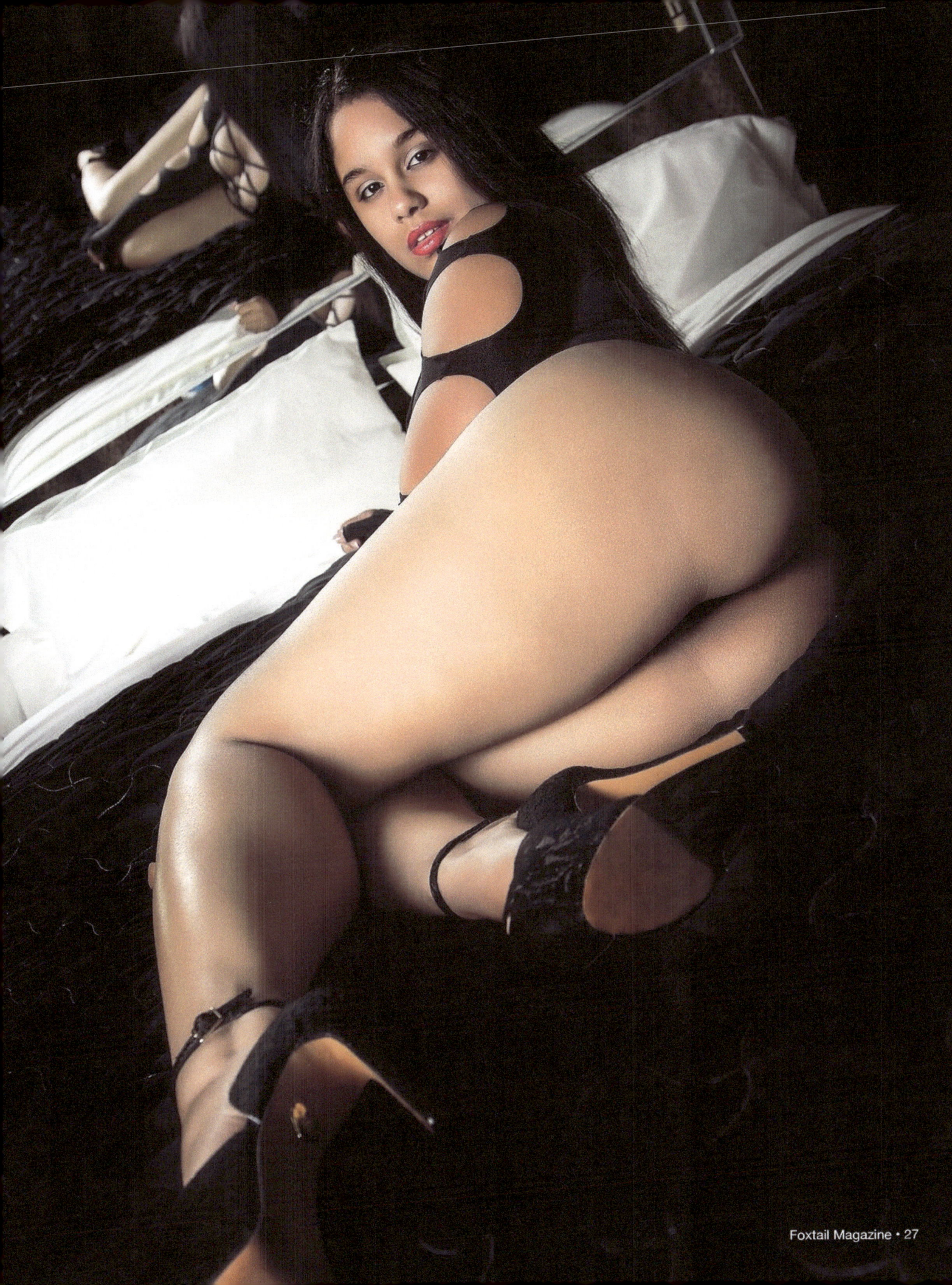

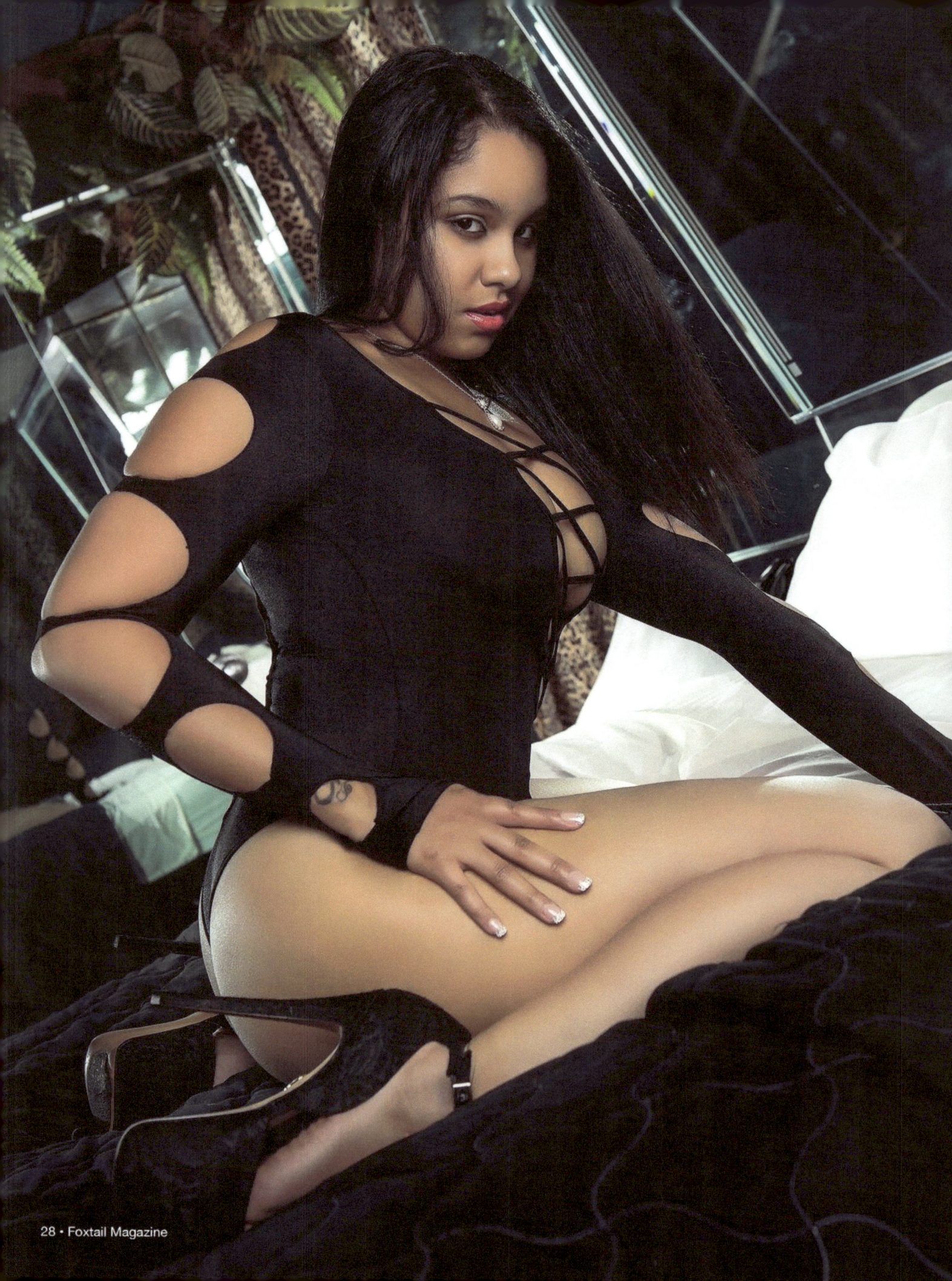

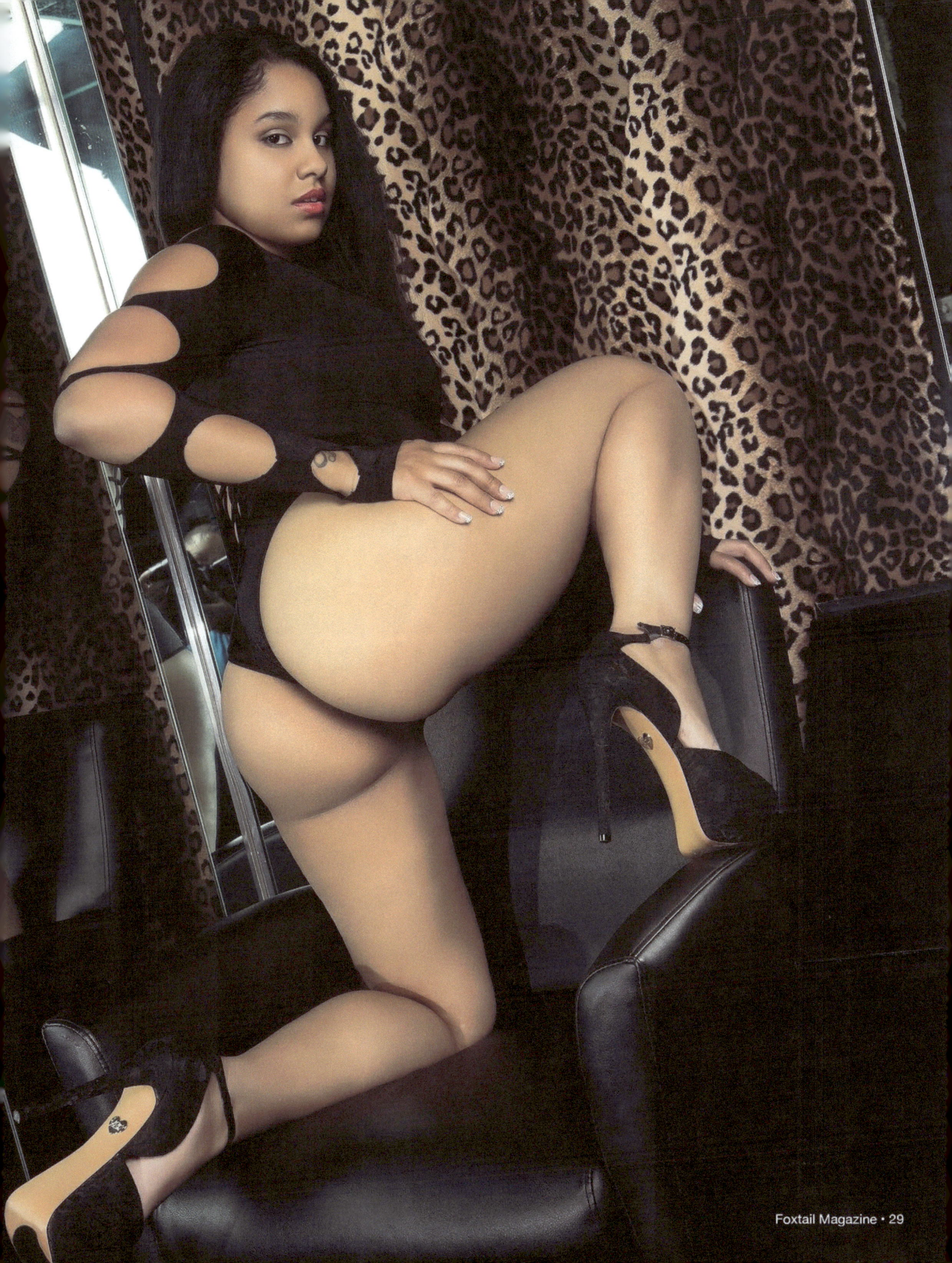

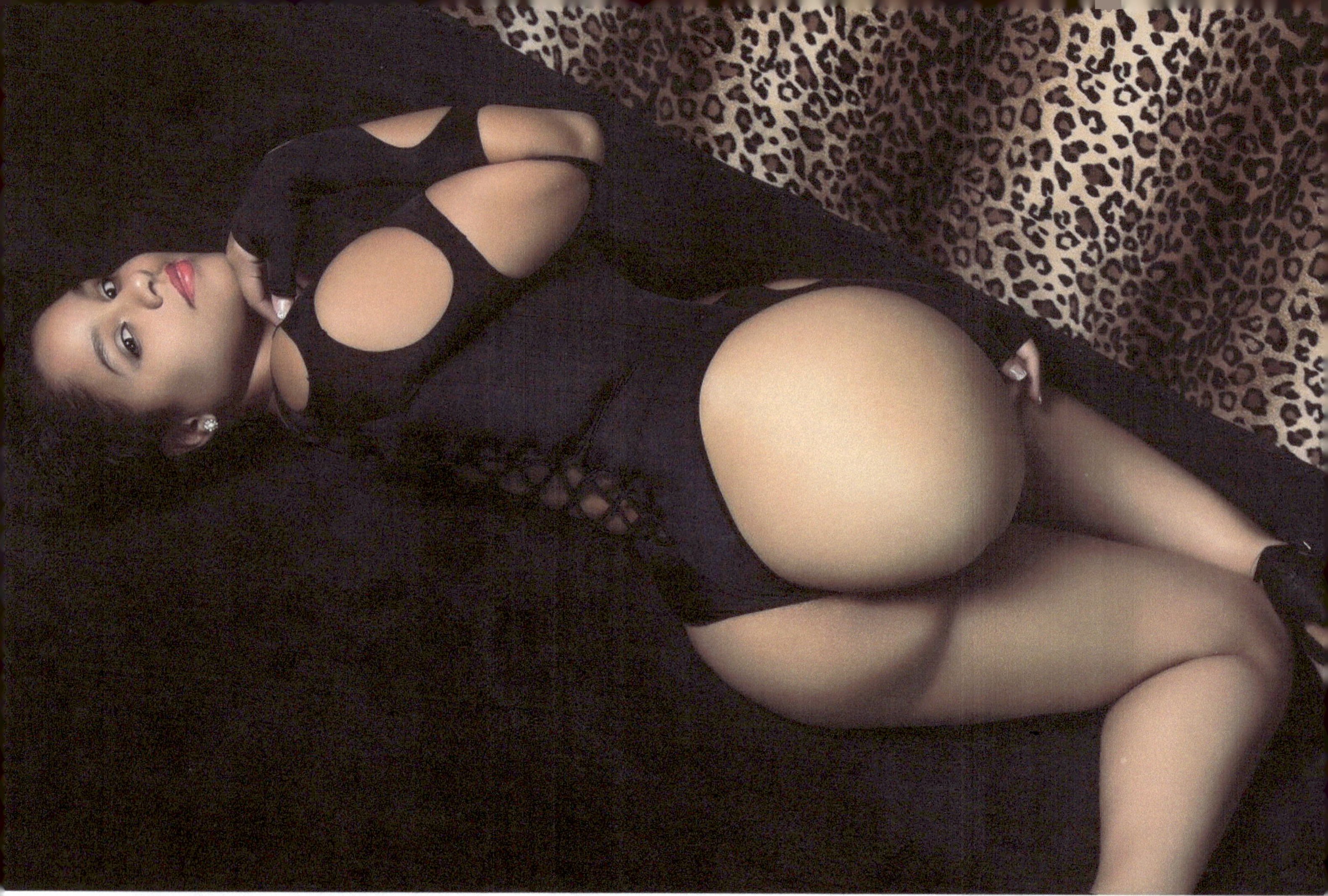

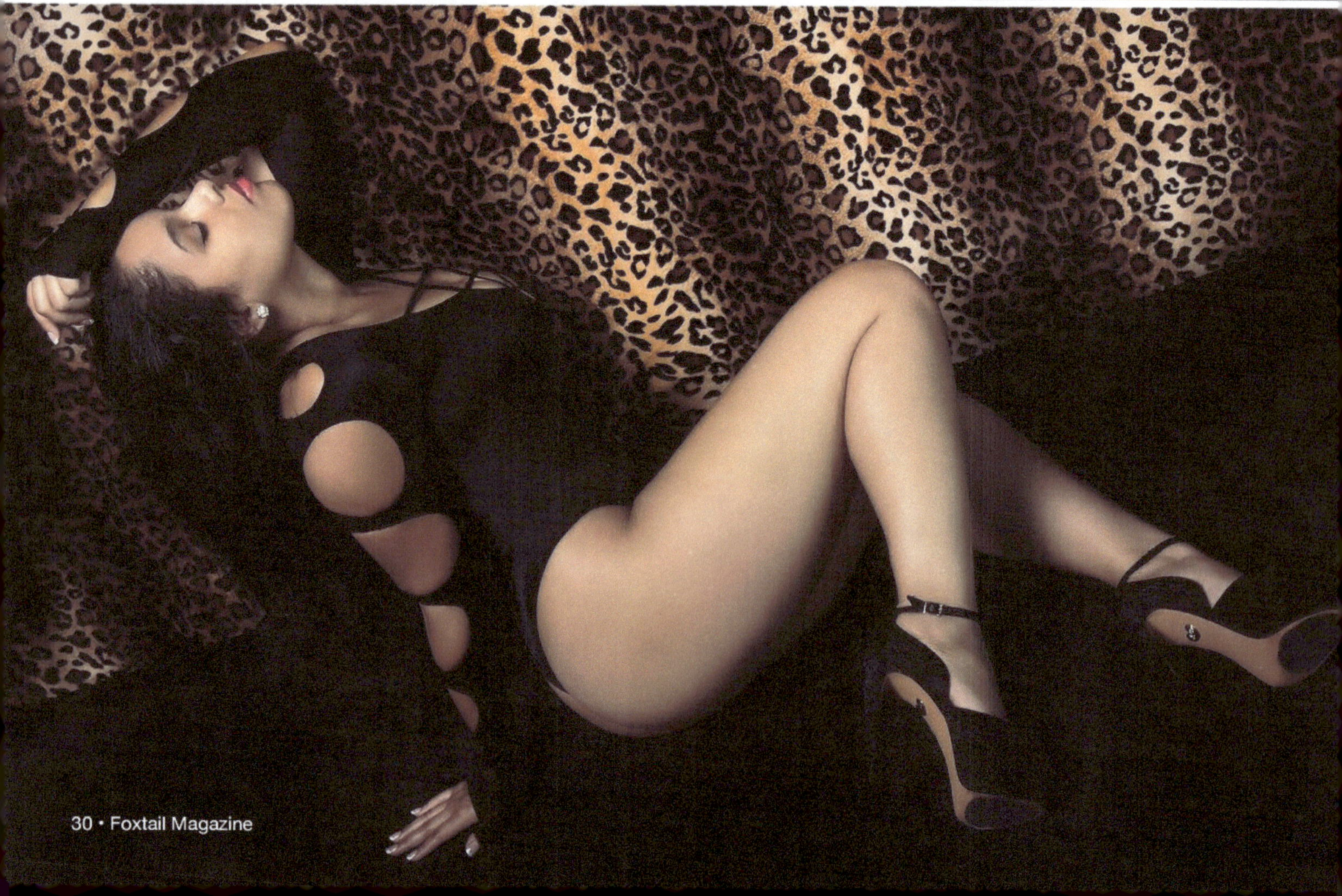

30 • Foxtail Magazine

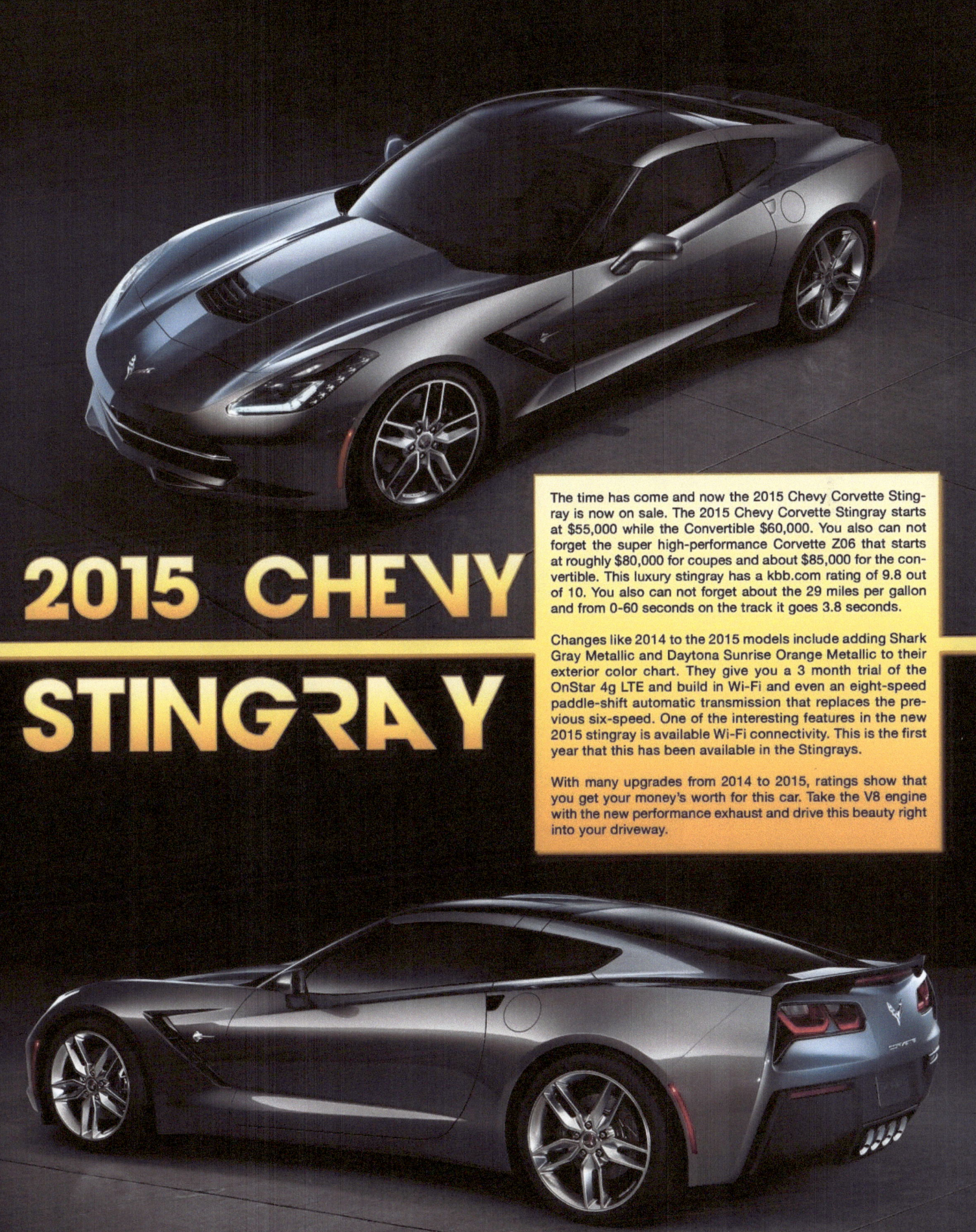

2015 CHEVY STINGRAY

The time has come and now the 2015 Chevy Corvette Stingray is now on sale. The 2015 Chevy Corvette Stingray starts at $55,000 while the Convertible $60,000. You also can not forget the super high-performance Corvette Z06 that starts at roughly $80,000 for coupes and about $85,000 for the convertible. This luxury stingray has a kbb.com rating of 9.8 out of 10. You also can not forget about the 29 miles per gallon and from 0-60 seconds on the track it goes 3.8 seconds.

Changes like 2014 to the 2015 models include adding Shark Gray Metallic and Daytona Sunrise Orange Metallic to their exterior color chart. They give you a 3 month trial of the OnStar 4g LTE and build in Wi-Fi and even an eight-speed paddle-shift automatic transmission that replaces the previous six-speed. One of the interesting features in the new 2015 stingray is available Wi-Fi connectivity. This is the first year that this has been available in the Stingrays.

With many upgrades from 2014 to 2015, ratings show that you get your money's worth for this car. Take the V8 engine with the new performance exhaust and drive this beauty right into your driveway.

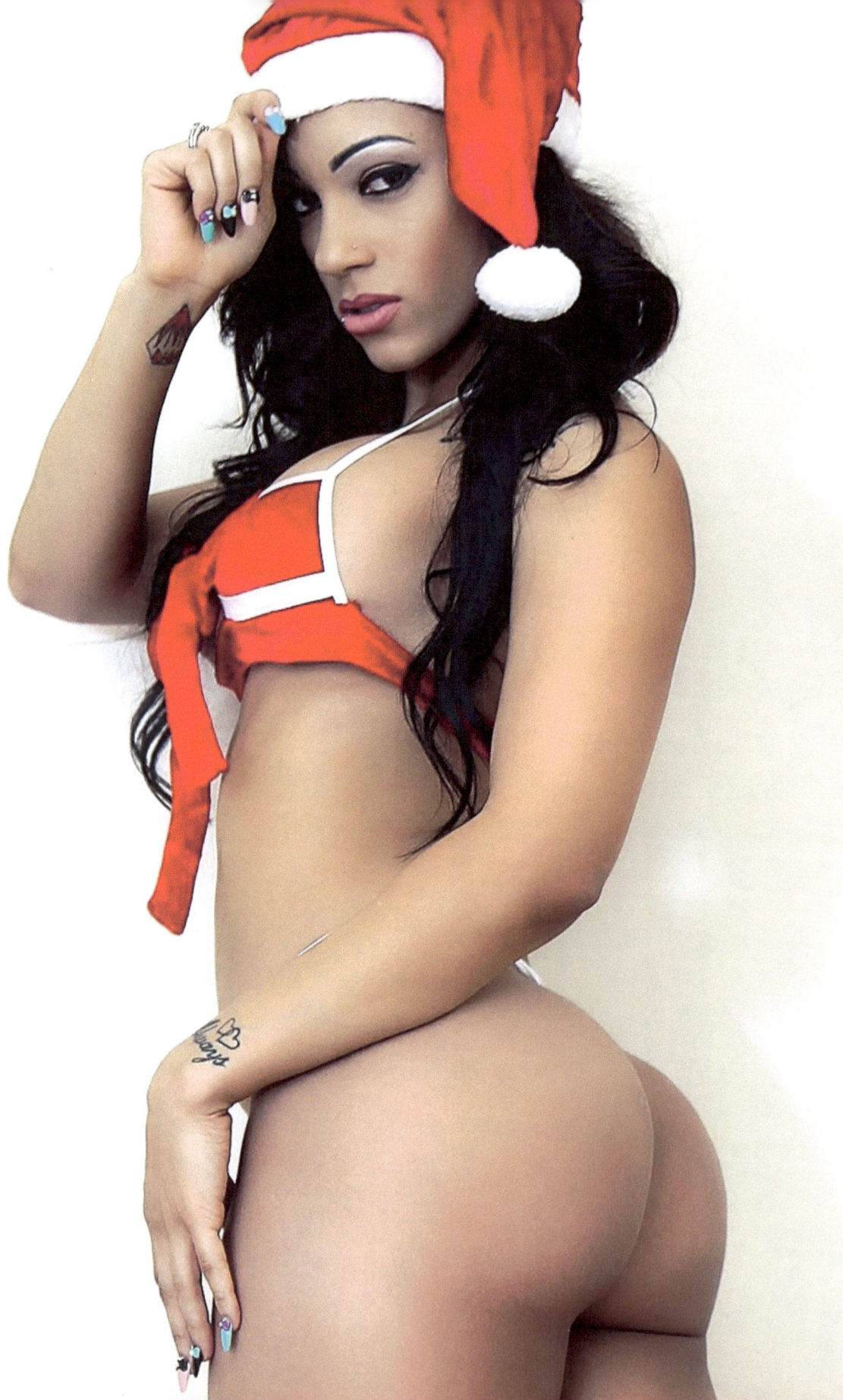

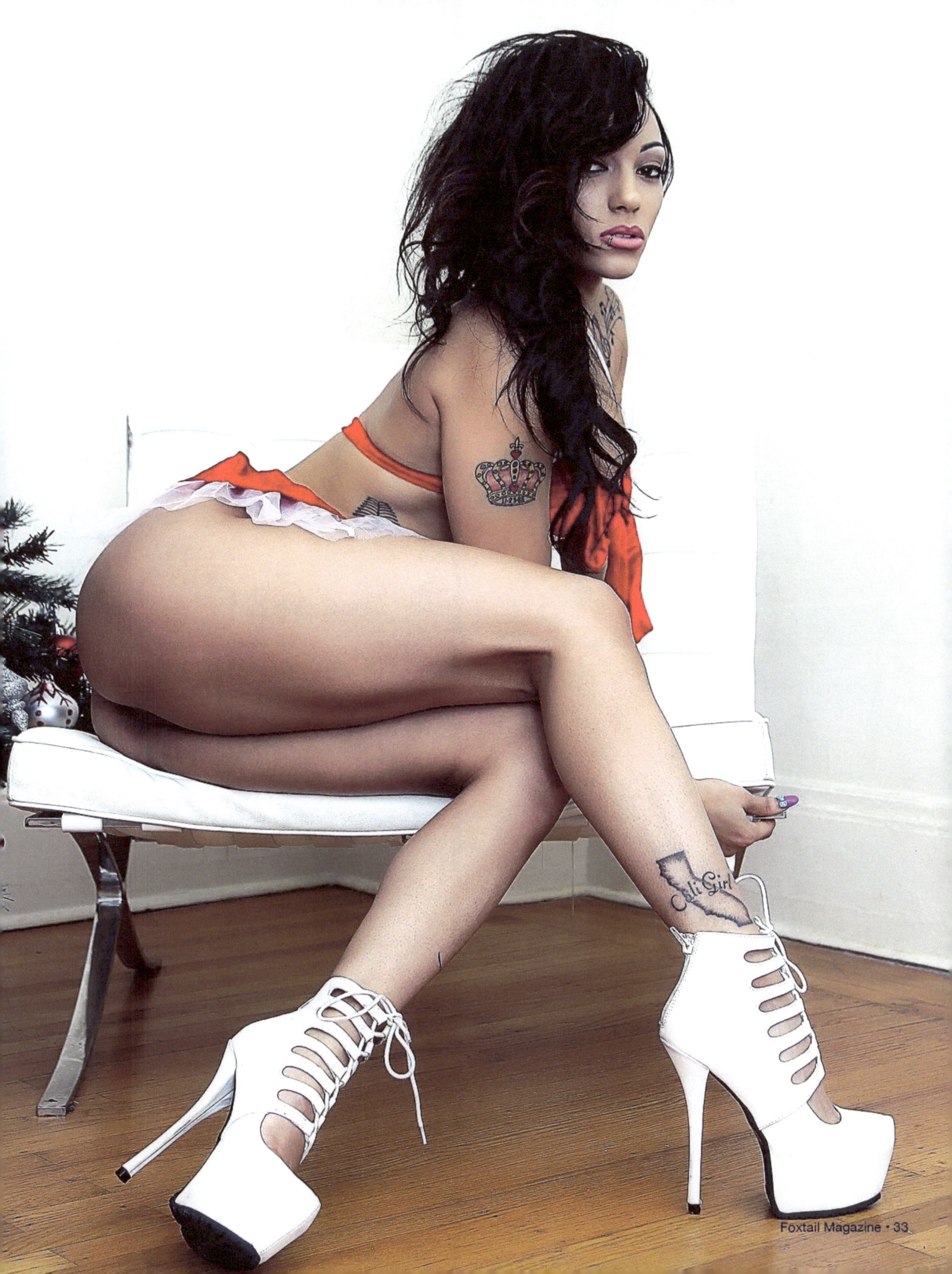

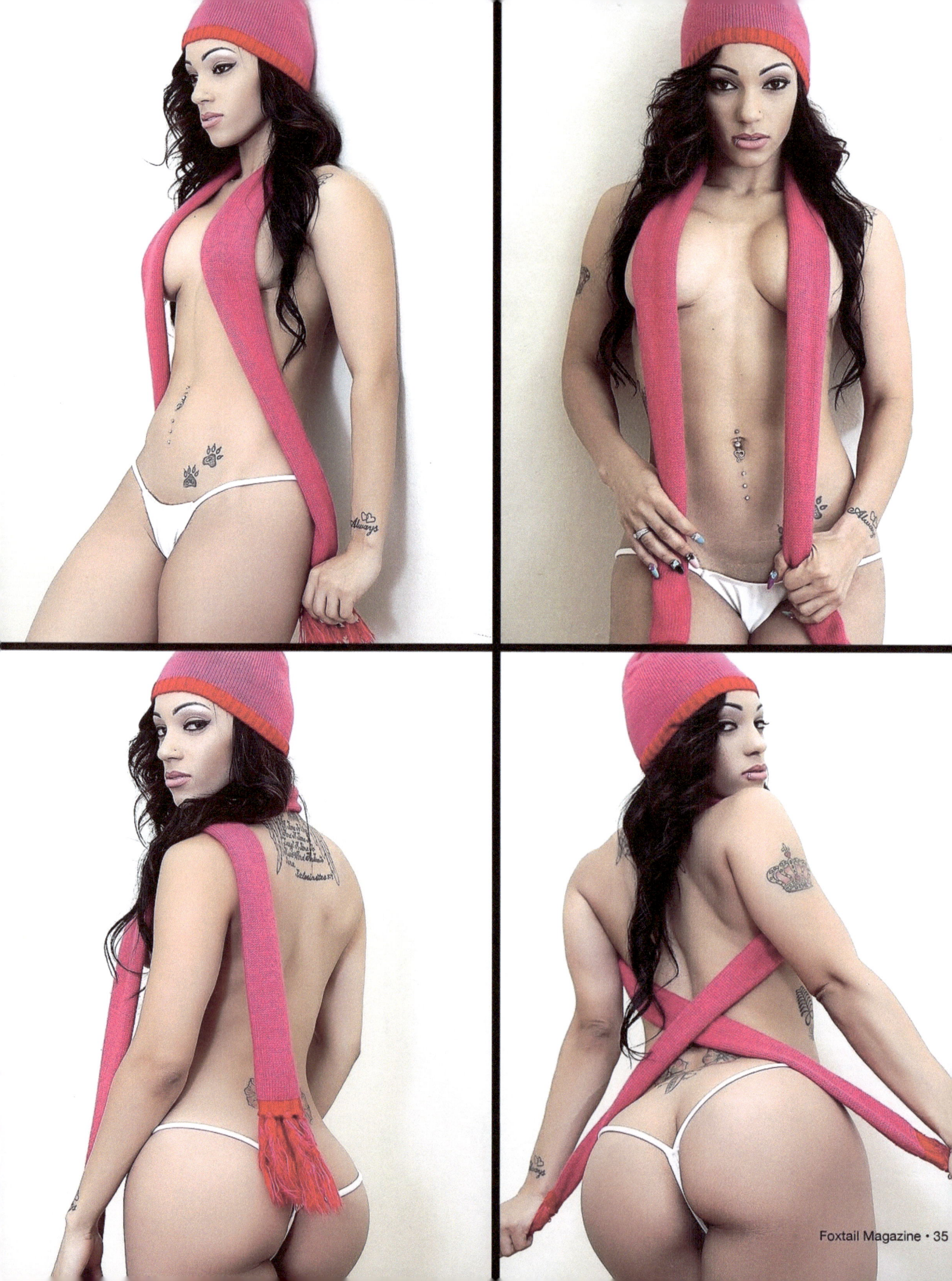

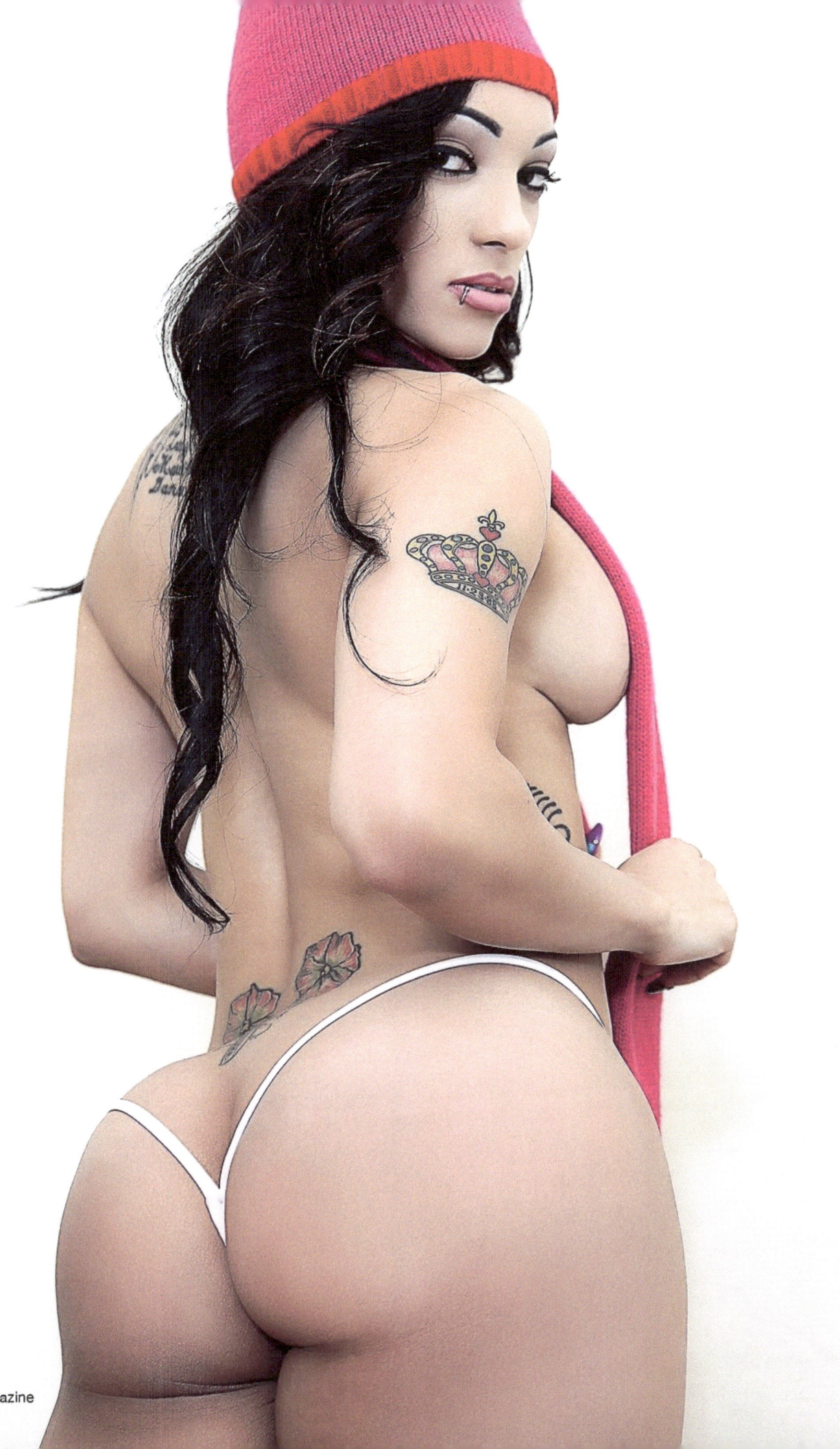

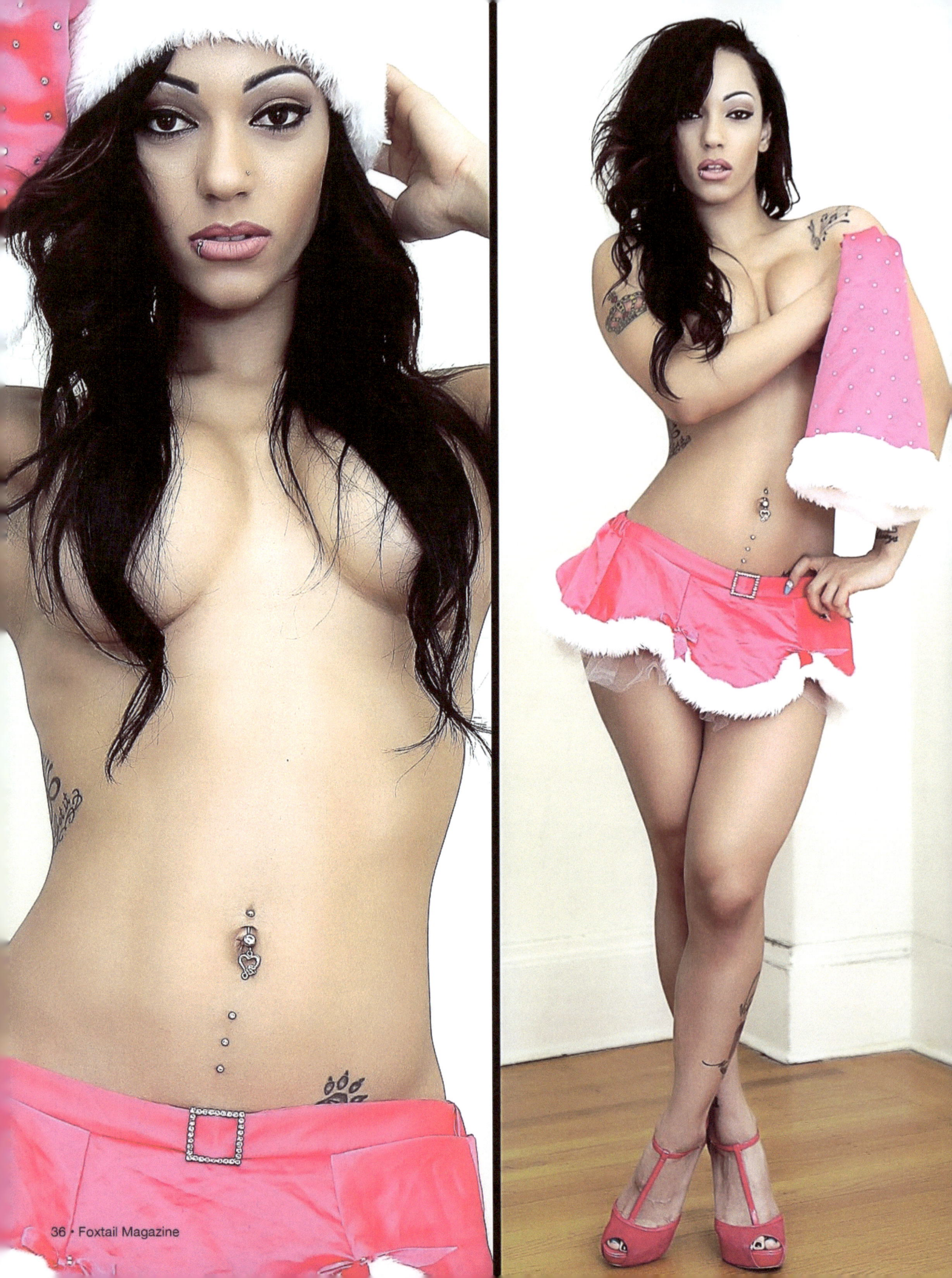

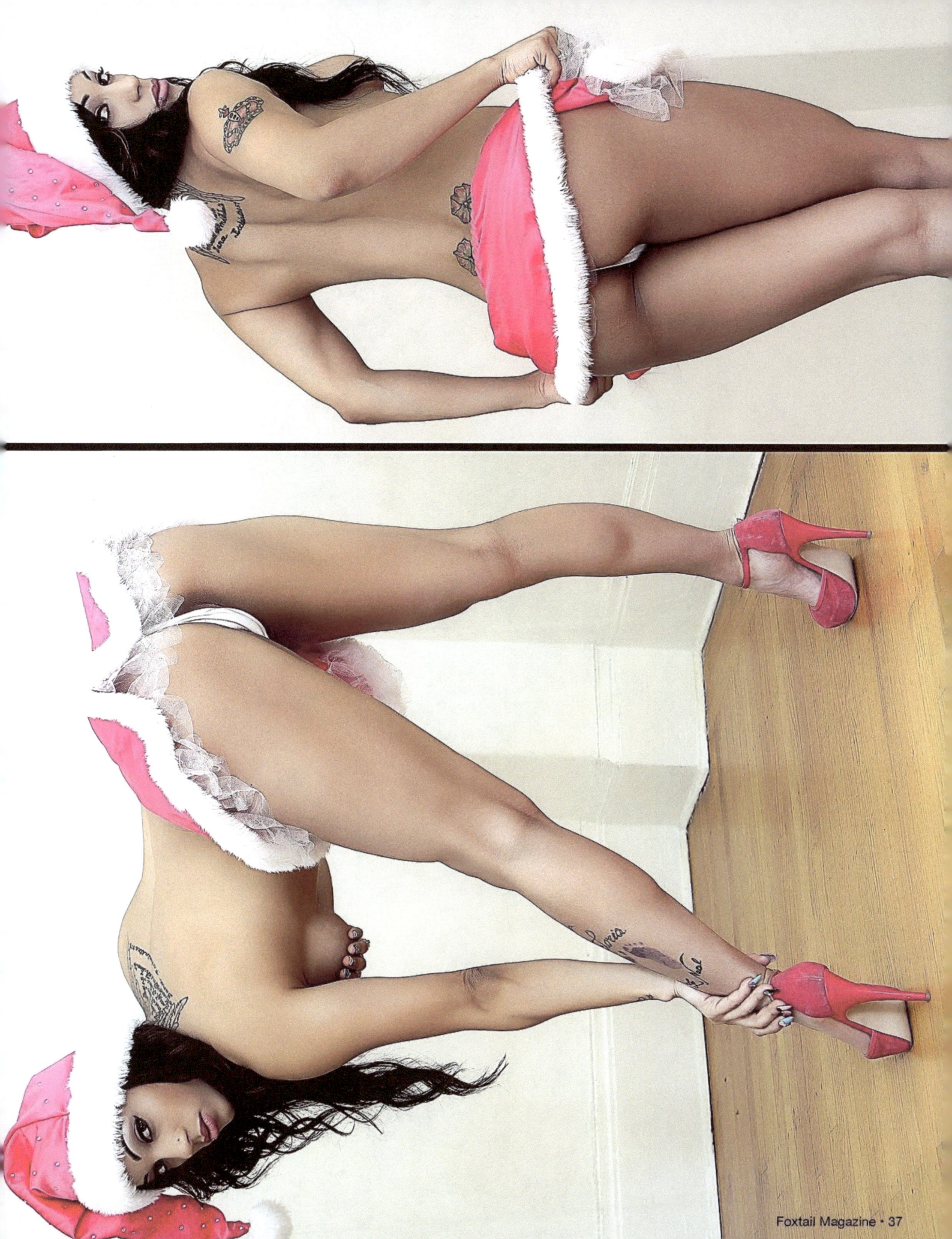

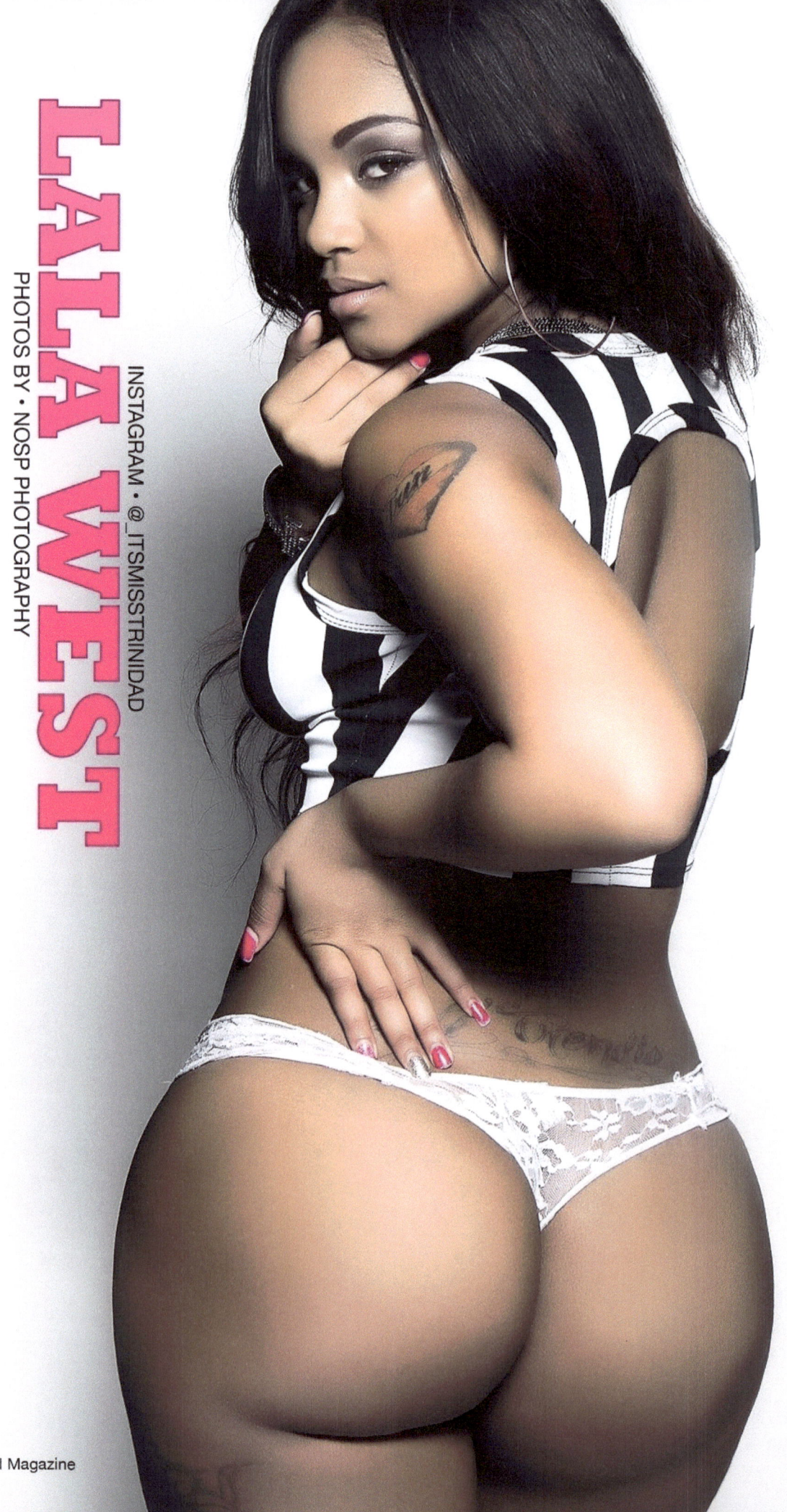

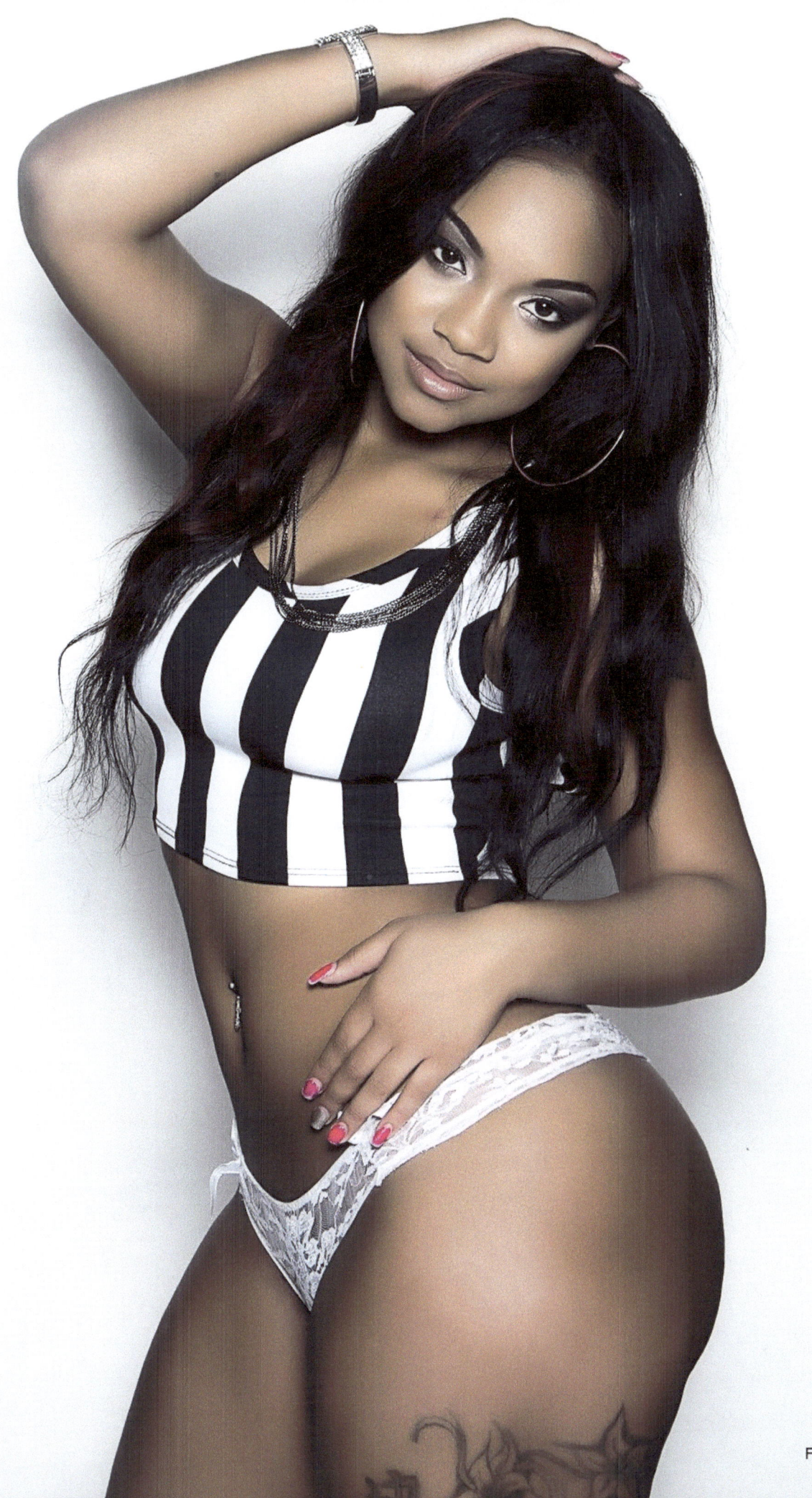

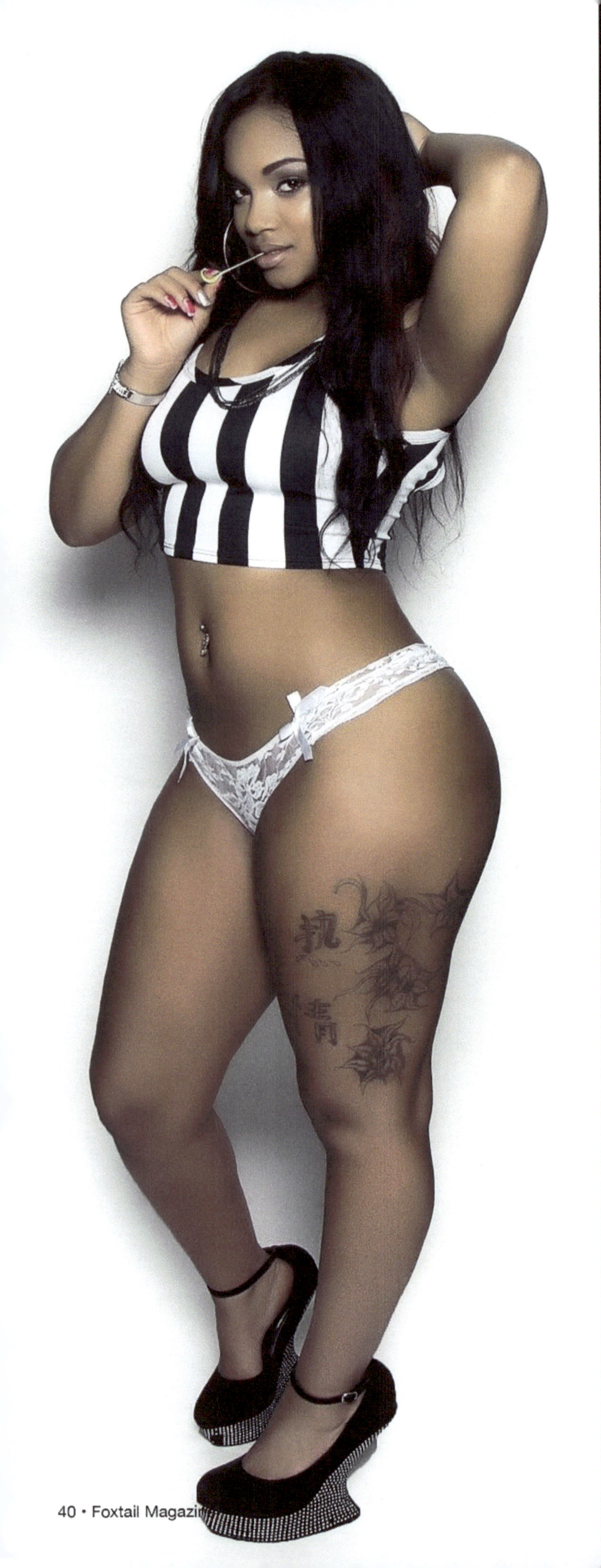

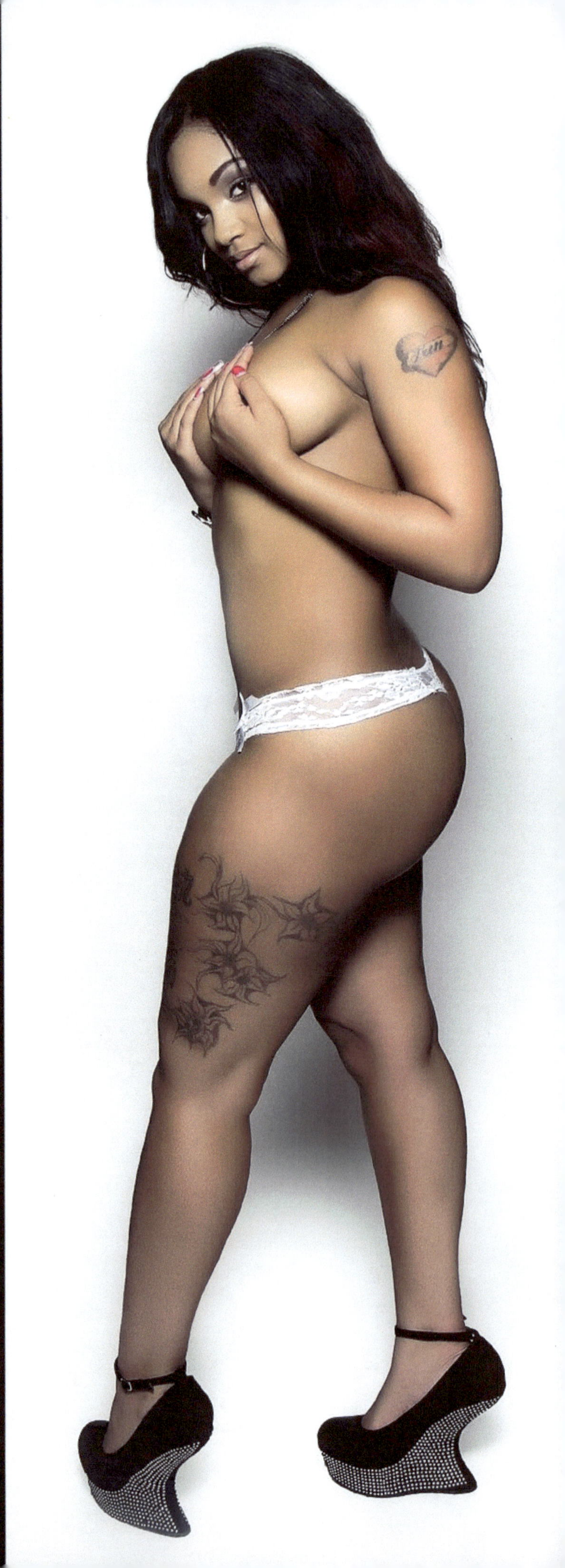

40 • Foxtail Magazine

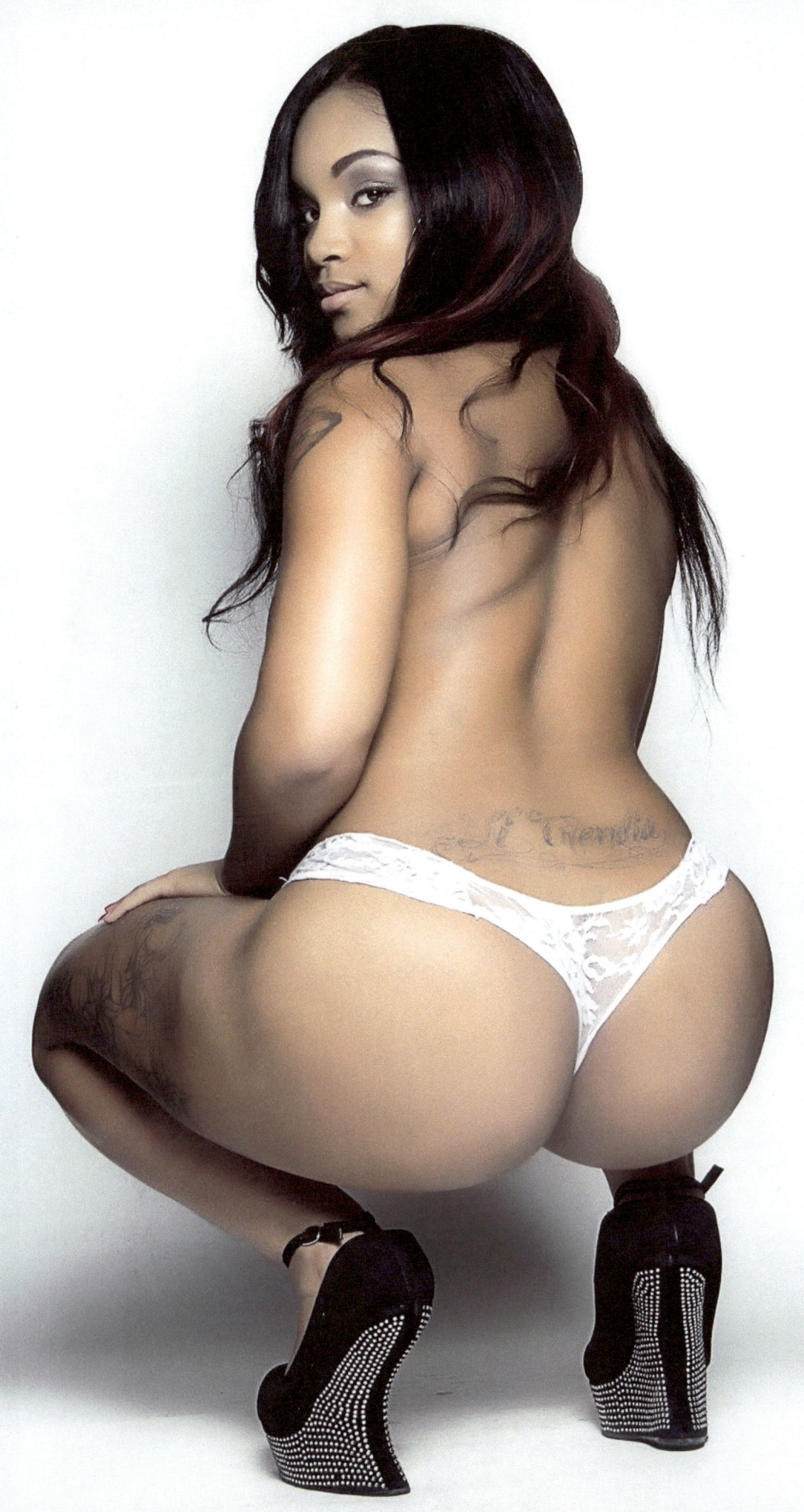

BELLA NYKOLE

PHOTOS BY • MYRON VINES PHOTOGRAPHY

INSTAGRAM • @THEONLYBELLANYKOLE

Height • 5'8" | Weight • 160 | Hair Color • Black | Eye Color • Brown | Measurements • 36C - 27 - 43

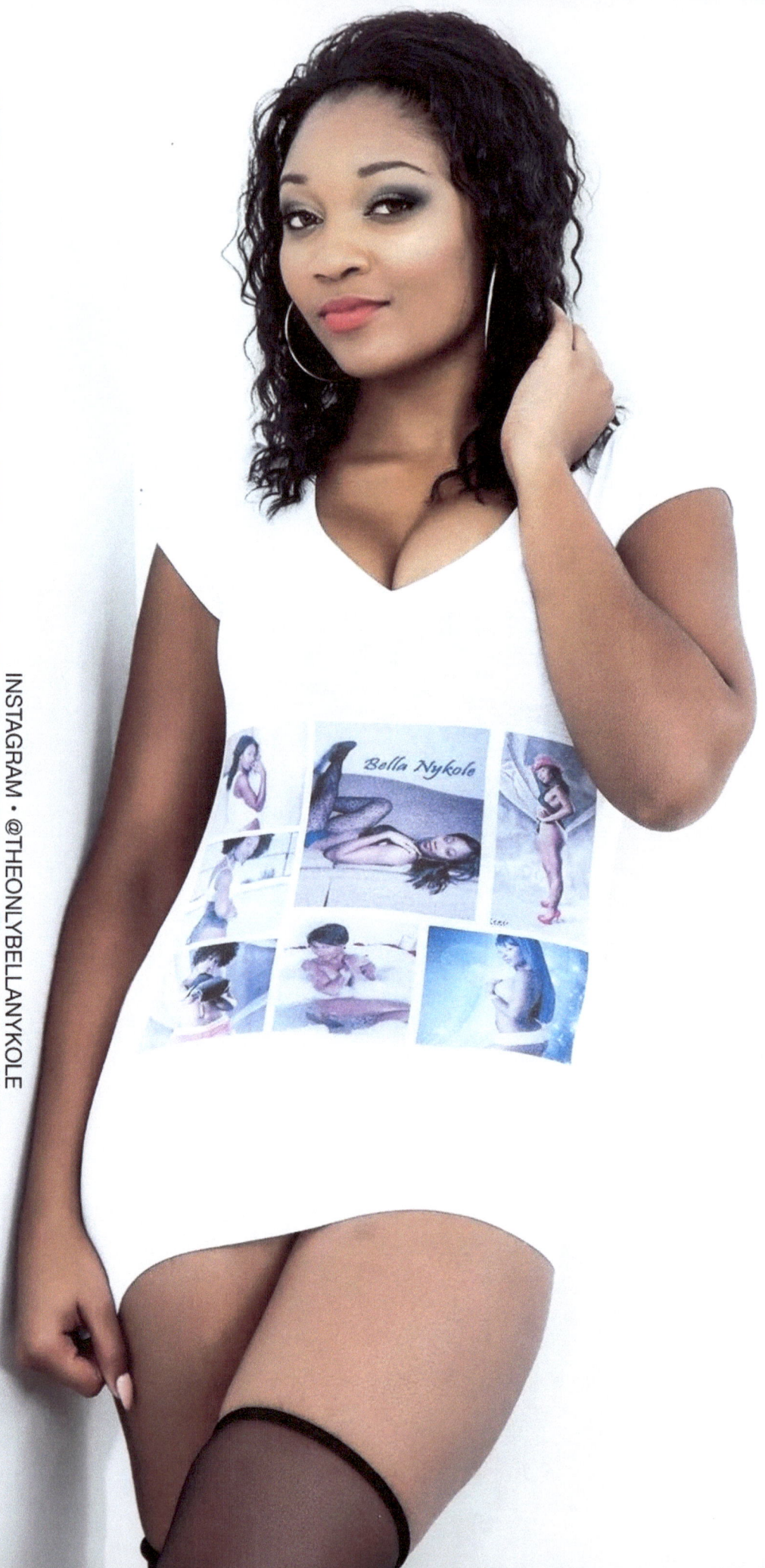

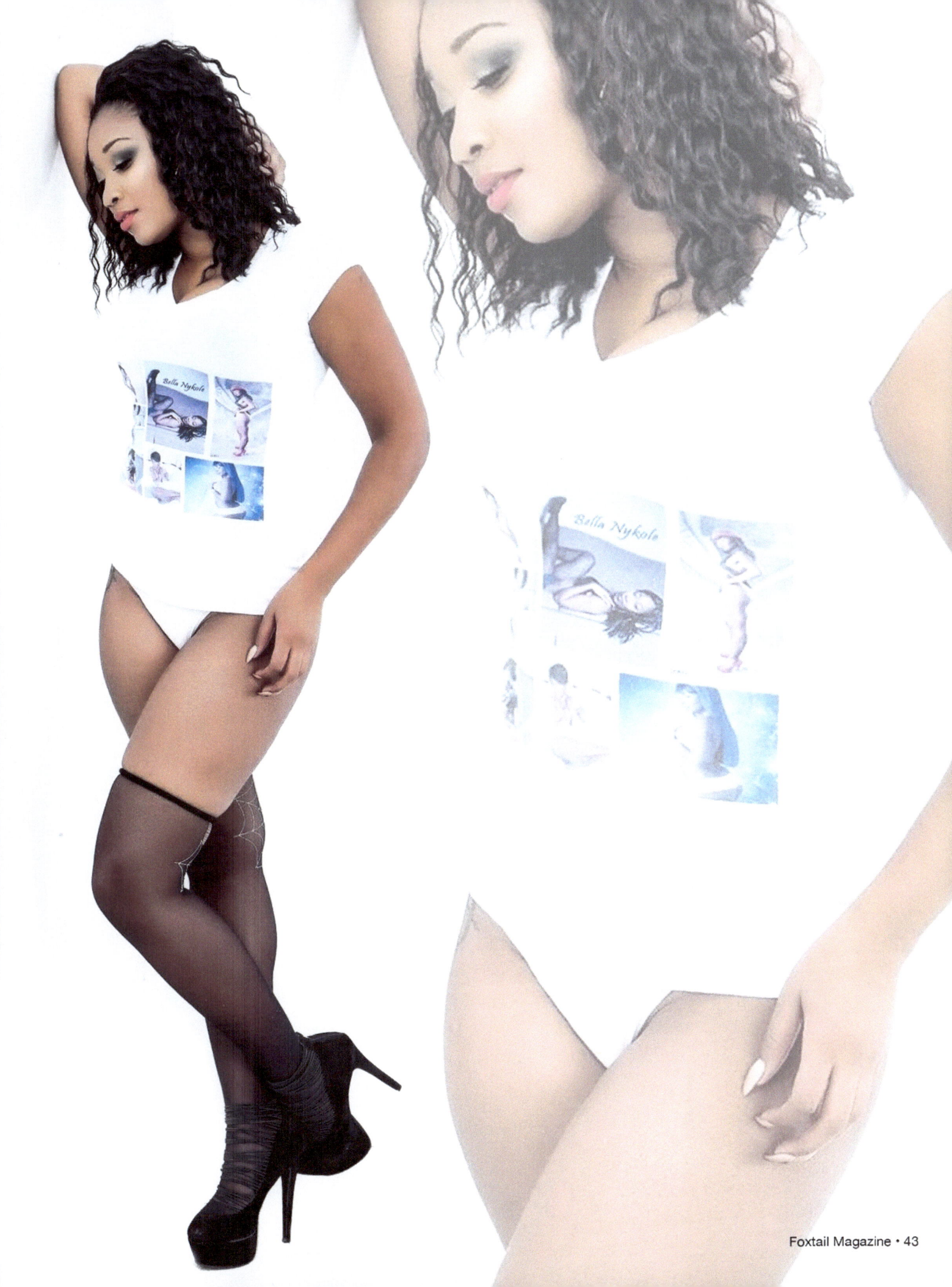

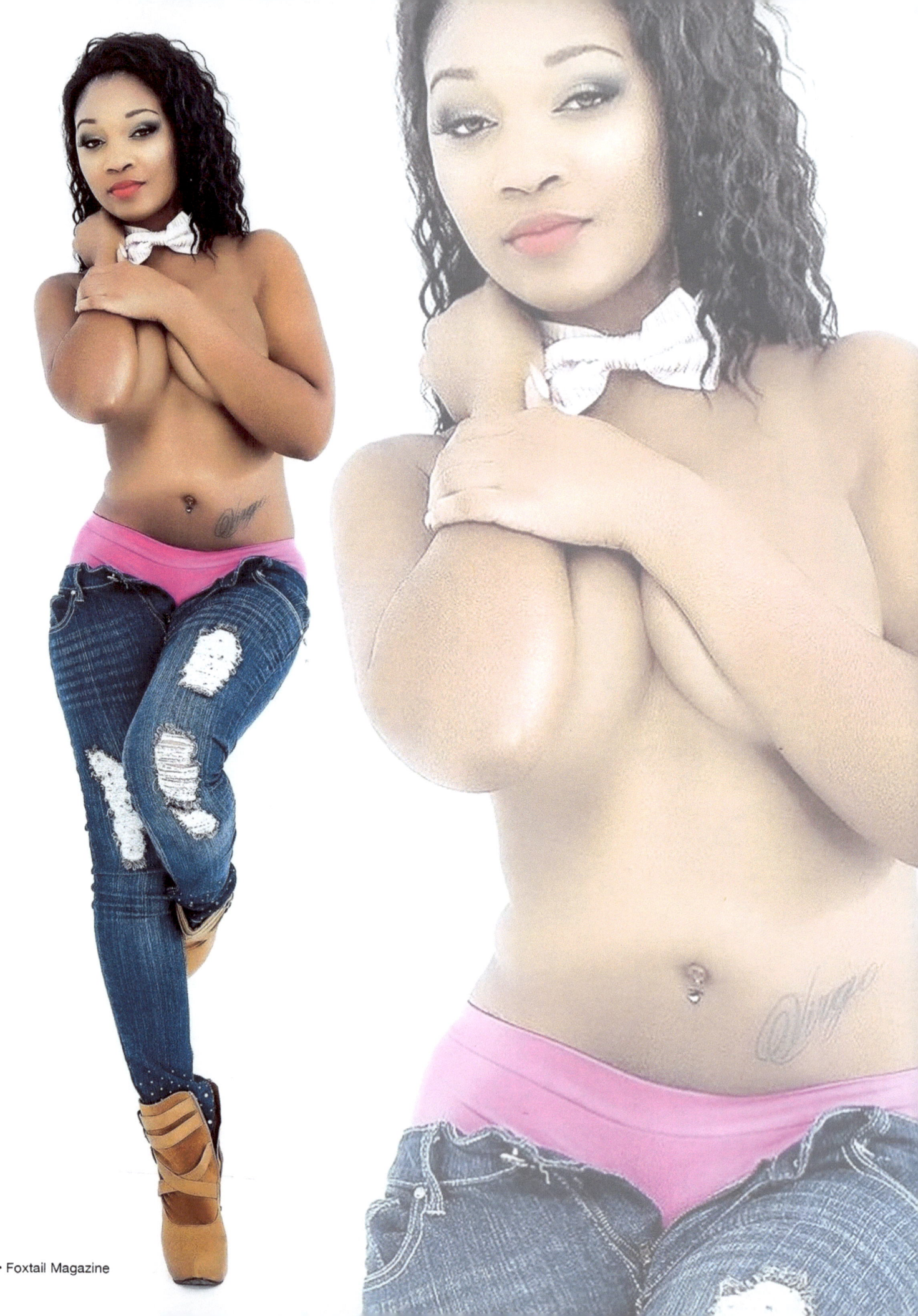

44 • Foxtail Magazine

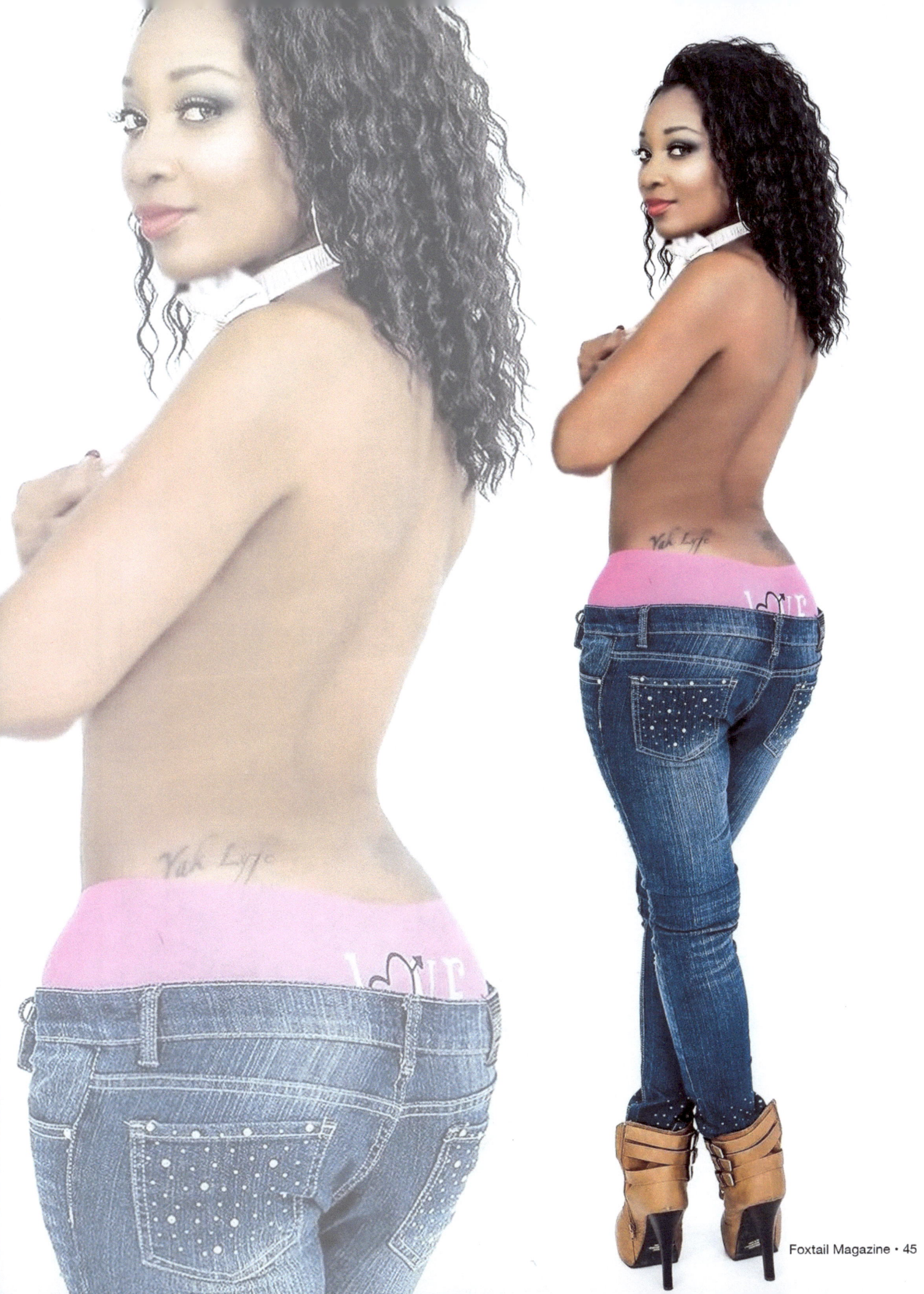

FOXTAIL OF THE MONTH

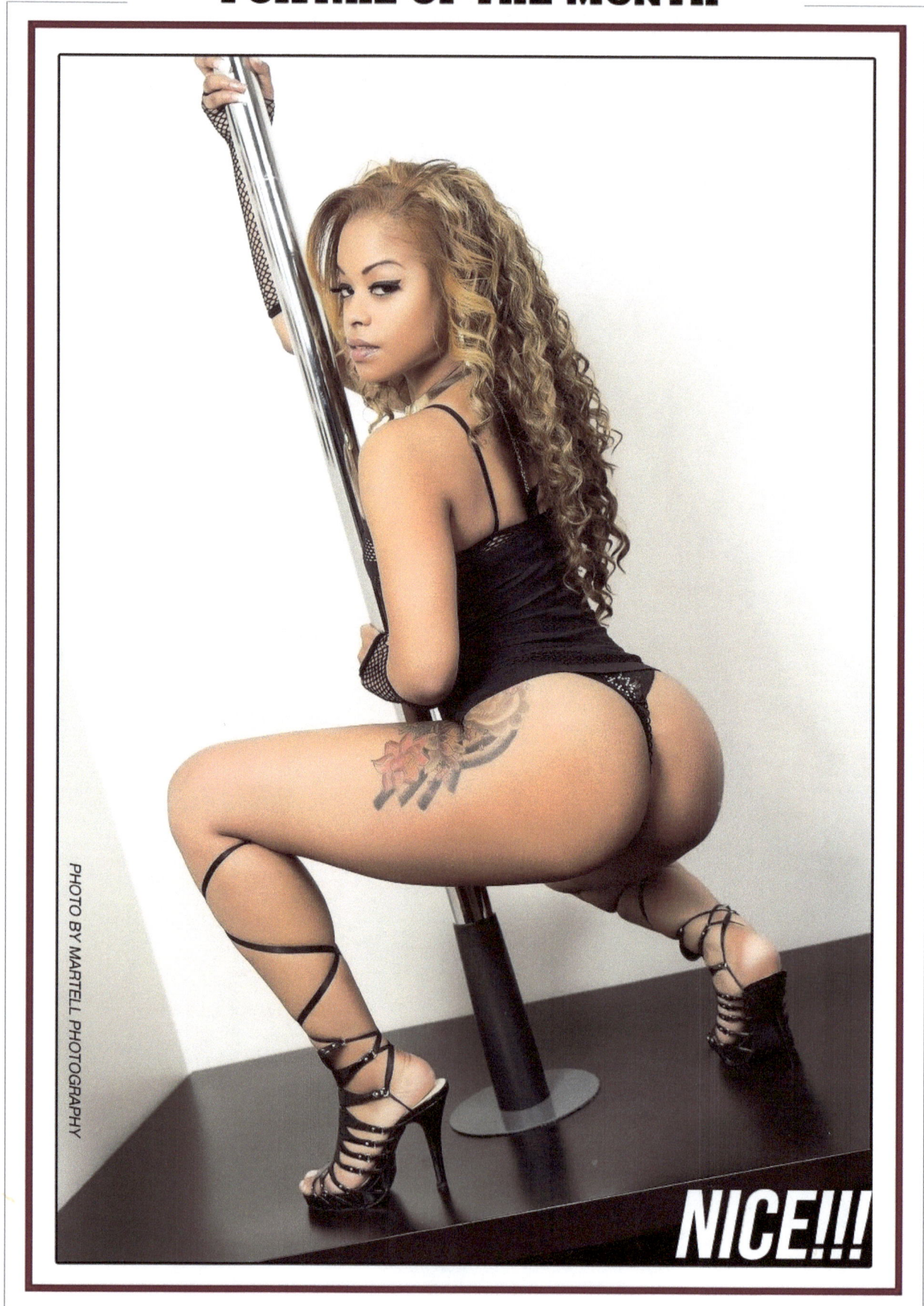

Miracle Vera • IG: *ur_miracl3*

GET **FOXTAIL** MAGAZINE
On the Devices that Matter to You the Most!!!

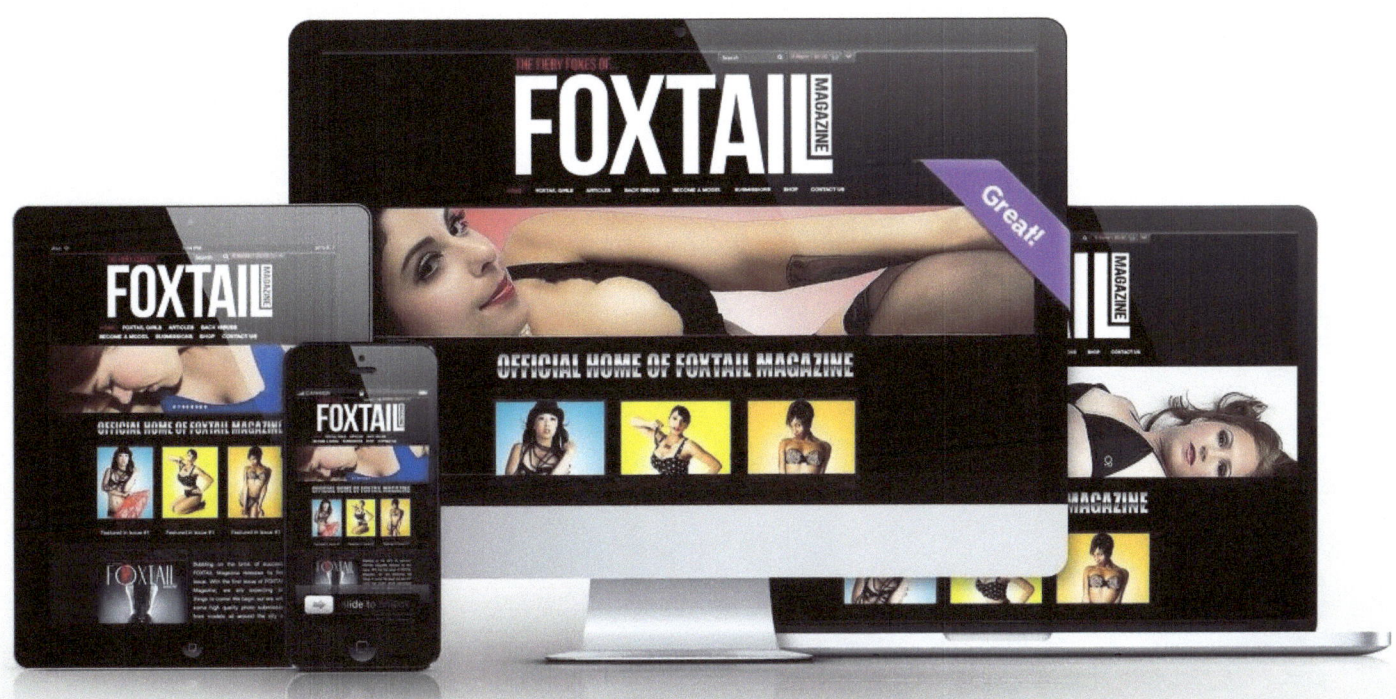

ADVERTISE
WITH
FOXTAIL MAGAZINE

FOR MORE INFOMATION, SEND EMAIL TO: ADVERTISING@FOXTAILMAG.COM

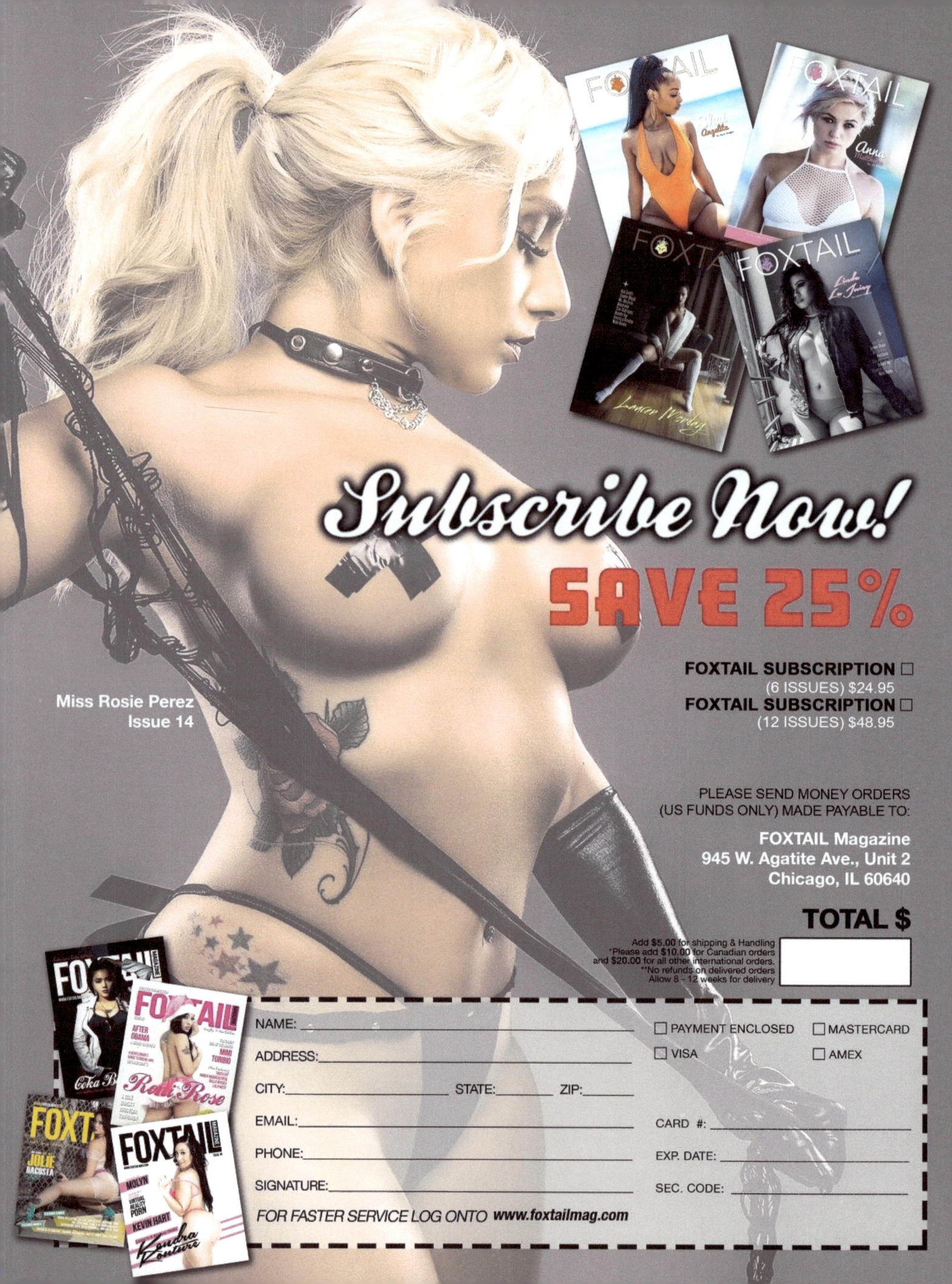

#TRENDING_NOW

STAY CONNECTED

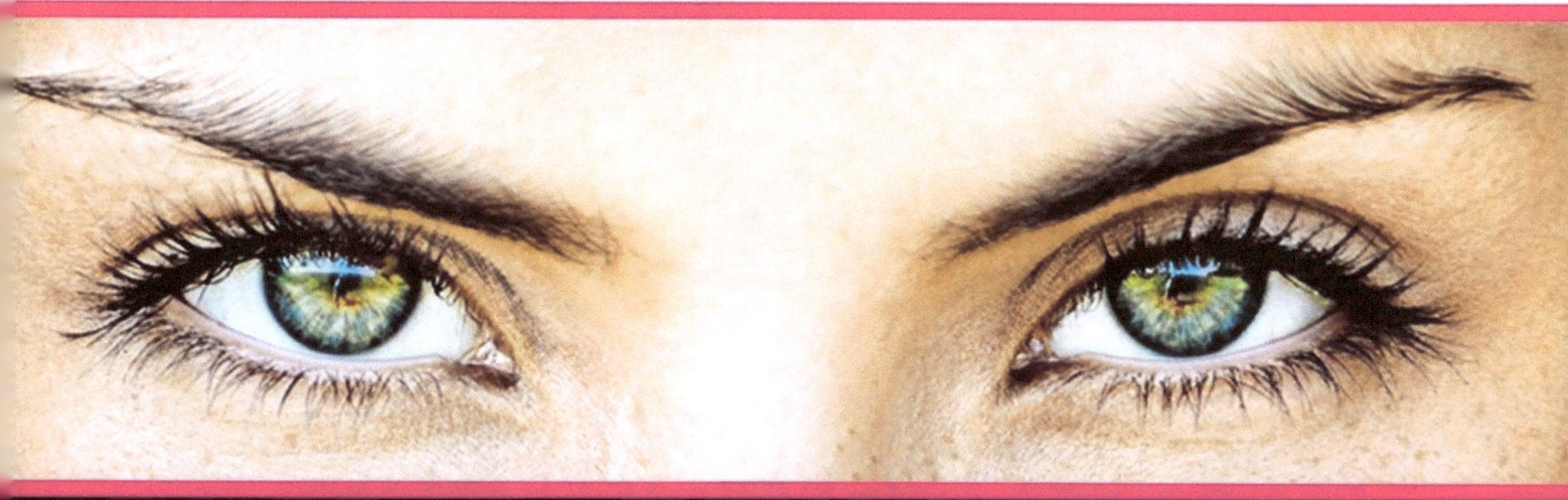

WITH
FOXTAIL MAGAZINE

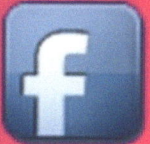 FACEBOOK.COM/FOXTAILMAGAZINE    INSTAGRAM.COM/FOXTAIL_MAGAZINE

 VIMEO.COM/FOXTAILMAGAZINE    TWITTER.COM/FOXTAIL_MAG

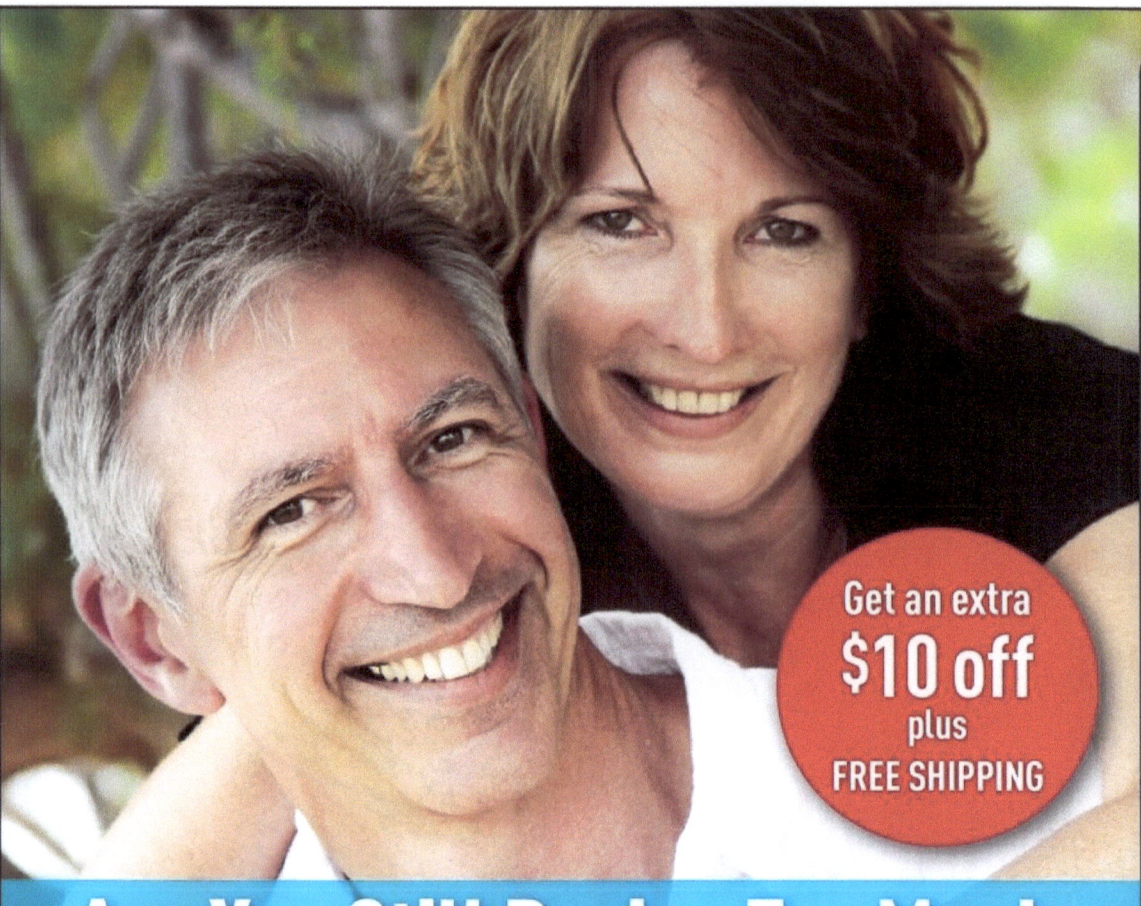

You can save up to **93%** when you fill your prescriptions with our Canadian and International prescription service.

Their Price
Celebrex™
$761.35
Typical US brand price for 200mg x 100

Our Price
Celecoxib*
$64.00
Generic equivalent of Celebrex™
Generic price for 200mg x 100

Get an extra **$10 off** plus **FREE SHIPPING**

Are You Still Paying Too Much For Your Medications?

Compare our prices and see how much you can save!
For more prices call us toll-free at **1-800-498-8263**

Nexium™ $841.81 **Esomeprazole* $78.00**
Typical US Brand Price for 40mg x 100 — Generic Price for 40mg x 100

Advair™ $938.10 vs **Salmeterol & Fluticasone Propionate* $155.00**
Typical US Brand Price for 250-50mcg x 180 doses — Generic Price for 50/250mcg x 180 doses

Actonel™ $734.58 **Risedronate* $44.00**
Typical US Brand Price for 35mg x 12 — Generic Price for 35mg x 12

Evista™ $694.32 **Raloxifene* $76.00**
Typical US Brand Price for 60mg x 100 — Generic Price for 60mg x 100

Save more today with an extra $10 off and free shipping!

Get an extra $10 off our first order today!

Call the number below and save an additional $10 plus get free shipping on your first prescription order with Canada Drug Center. Expires June 30, 2015. Offer is valid for prescription orders only and can not be used in conjunction with any other offers. Valid for new customers only. One time use per household.
Use code 10FREE to receive this special offer.

Order Now! Toll-free: 1-800-498-8263

Please note that we do not carry controlled substances and a valid prescription is required for all prescription medication orders.

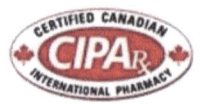 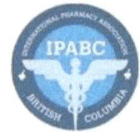 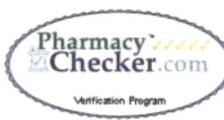 

Prescription price comparison above is valid as of November 1, 2014. All trade-mark (TM) rights associated with the brand name products in this ad belong to their respective owners. *Generic drugs are carefully regulated medications that have the same active ingredients as the original brand name drug, but are generally cheaper in price.

www.ingramcontent.com/pod-product-compliance
Lightning Source LLC
Chambersburg PA
CBHW051215220526
45473CB00003B/1045